Welcoming The Stranger

*Practising Hospitality
in Contemporary Ireland*

Edited by
Andrew G. McGrady

First published 2006 by
Veritas Publications
7/8 Lower Abbey Street
Dublin 1
Ireland
Email publications@veritas.ie
Website www.veritas.ie

10 9 8 7 6 5 4 3 2 1

ISBN 1 85390 932 7
978 1 85390 932 0 (from January 2007)

A catalogue record for this book is available from the British Library.

Scripture quotations from the *New Revised Standard Version Bible* © 1993 and 1998 by the Division of Christian Education of the National Churches of Christ in the United States of America, except p. 98, *The New Jerusalem Bible* © 1985 and 1990 by Darton, Longman & Todd, Ltd.

The lines from Robert Frost's 'The Death of a Hired Man' are taken from *The Poetry of Robert Frost: The Collected Poems*, courtesy of Henry Holt and Co., 1969.

'Love after Love' by Derek Walcott is taken from *Seagrapes*, courtesy of Farrar, Straus & Sons, 1976.

Cover image © Getty Images, 2006

Designed and typeset by Paula Ryan
Printed in the Republic of Ireland by Betaprint, Dublin

Veritas books are printed on paper made from the wood pulp of managed forests. For every tree felled, at least one tree is planted, thereby renewing natural resources.

Contents

I was a Stranger and You made Me Welcome

Andrew G. McGrady

Introduction
The papers in this volume flow mainly from a conference organised by the Institute of Hospitality of the Hospitaller Order of St John of God and held in Dublin in June 2005. The Order is dedicated to the provision of social, education, welfare and health services. In Ireland, St John of God Hospitaller Services provides mental health services, care for older people and services for children and adults with disabilities. The Province also manages programmes in Malawi, Africa and New Jersey, USA. Each year up to 3,000 individuals receive support through services operated by over 2,000 staff and volunteers, including thirty-six members of the Order. The Institute of Hospitality aims to promote the core philosophy of the Order, namely that people are the creation of God, with intrinsic value and inherent dignity. This philosophy is based on the beliefs and values of the Order's founder, St John of God.

St John of God
In 1537 in the Spanish city of Granada a man named John was struggling to put his life back together after spending a period as a patient in the psychiatric wing of a hospital. His precise surname is unknown but he was a bookseller and his origins may have been in present day Portugal. Homeless and disillusioned after leaving the hospital, he felt a strong desire to improve the situation of the many men, women and children who, like himself, were marginalised. John began to bring those who were sick and weak and those unable to cope to share his humble accommodation on the porch of the house of a friend. In the beginning he was regarded by his fellow citizens as the crazy madman John who acted so strangely in the streets of their city. But as his work took hold of the imagination of his neighbours,

they began to see him as 'God's John'. This sharing of life was the stark and simple beginning of the work which today still bears his name. When the Brothers of St John of God were founded in the 1570s to carry on his work, the word they used to describe John's vision and mission was 'hospitality'. This they defined as 'welcoming the stranger'. St John of God Services has continued to strive to carry this love, care and compassion to people down the centuries. Hospitality is the name given to this great gift of care and welcome first given by 'God's John' to the poor, the homeless, the sick and the dying and many others in the city of Granada over 460 years ago.

In recent times, the St John of God family has discovered that it is by no means alone in its exploration of hospitality as a spiritual vision and has realised that it is a challenging reality of profound relevance for our times. Hospitality is about creating ever-widening circles of inclusion and participation. Across the world today the marginalised and the homeless, including those with learning disabilities, refugees, asylum seekers and economic migrants, still huddle for shelter in the doorways of affluence. They are the strangers in our midst and they call on our hospitality. The papers in this book explore this ever-insistent call to hospitality.

In his chapter, 'The Jericho Road', Fr Fintan Brennan-Whitmore OH (the Provincial of the Irish Province of the Brothers of St John of God), explores the parable of the Good Samaritan as a paradigm of the 'Gospel of hospitality' and the basis of a 'rule of life'. Brennan-Whitmore argues that placing a value on hospitality means being open to changing our priorities to respond to the unexpected human needs of others and living life in a way that is open to whatever happens while we are trying to do something altogether different. This means believing in our heart of hearts that responding to the basic needs of a fellow human being should take precedence over all other considerations.

Welcoming the Migrant
While they may be aware of the increasing diversity of immigrants in today's 'Celtic Tiger' Ireland, most Irish people are totally unaware of

the wider picture that this represents, namely that recent decades are characterised by huge movements of human populations right across the globe. In recent years, over two hundred million migrants have moved either within or between countries, constituting the largest movement of people in human history.

There is a long tradition within the Catholic Church of a concern to welcome migrants. In approaching the pastoral care of migrants the Church is motivated by the words of Jesus who said, 'I was a stranger and you made me welcome' (Mt 25:35). In 1912, the first Office for Migration Problems was set up within the Vatican. In 1952 Pope Pius XII issued the Apostolic Constitution *Exsul familia* which systematically and globally addressed the pastoral care of migrants. In *Gaudium et spes* the Second Vatican Council also expressed its concern, calling on Christians to be aware of the phenomenon of migration. It reaffirmed the right to emigrate (GS 65), the dignity of migrants (GS 66), the need to overcome inequalities in economic and social development (GS 63) and to provide an answer to the authentic needs of the human person (GS 84). It also recognised the right of the public authorities to regulate the flow of migration (GS 87). In 1967, following the Council, Pope Paul VI issued his encyclical *Populorum progressio* (On the Development of Peoples) which included a consideration of both the causes and experience of migration. In 1969 Pope Paul VI issued his Motu proprio *Pastoralis migratorum Cura* promulgating the Instruction *De Pastorali migratorum Cura* and in 1970 he instituted the Pontifical Commission for the Pastoral Care of Migration and Tourism. In 1978 this Pontifical Commission addressed a circular letter to Episcopal Conferences entitled 'The Church and Human Mobility'. In 1988, following the issuing by Pope John Paul II of the Apostolic Constitution *Pastor bonus*, the Commission became the Pontifical Council for the Pastoral Care of Migrants and Itinerant People which in 2004 issued the most recent document *Erga migrantes caritas Christi* (The love of Christ towards Migrants, EMCC). It should also be noted that all popes since Paul VI have issued messages for the World Days of Migrants and Refugees, which have repeatedly affirmed the fundamental rights of the person.

The migration we are experiencing today is an expression of globalisation which has 'flung markets wide open, but not frontiers, has demolished boundaries for the free circulation of information and capital, but not to the same extent those for the free circulation of people' (EMCC par. 4). Migration on such a massive scale poses fundamental ethical problems, related to the establishment of a new international economic order based upon a just and equitable distribution of the goods of the earth. Migration is 'a clear indication of social, economic and demographic imbalance on a regional or world-wide level, which drives people to emigrate' (EMCC par. 1). A more just economic order 'would make a real contribution to reducing and checking the flow of a large number of migrants from populations in difficulty' (EMCC par. 8). The phenomenon of migration thus calls for us to redefine our understanding of the international community and to see humanity as a family of peoples in which the answer to 'who is my neighbour?' is simply 'everyone'. Unfortunately, the response to the migrant is often not one of welcome; rather 'the precarious situation of so many foreigners, which should arouse everyone's solidarity, instead brings about fear in many, who feel that immigrants are a burden, regard them with suspicion and even consider them a danger and a threat' (EMCC 6). A different ethic of solidarity and outreach is needed since 'the migrant thirsts for some gesture that will make him feel welcome, recognised and acknowledged as a person' (EMCC 96). Within each local and regional society, what is required is not the exploitation or cultural assimilation of migrants, but rather what Pope John Paul II referred to as 'intercultural integration'. This more than 'an assimilation that leads migrants to suppress or to forget their own cultural identity. Rather, contact with others leads to discovering their "secret", to being open to them in order to welcome their valid aspects and thus contribute to knowing each one better'. There is a need for a 'dialogue between people of different cultures in a context of pluralism that goes beyond mere tolerance and reaches sympathy'.[1]

Migration also poses a uniquely religious challenge since many societies, including Ireland, are becoming increasingly pluralist with regard to religion. This requires of religious communities an ecumenical vision and underpins the need for inter-religious dialogue because an increasing number of migrants in traditionally Catholic countries belong to other religions. 'Migration thus offers the Church an historic opportunity to prove its four characteristic marks: the Church is *one* because in a certain sense it also expresses the unity of the whole human family; it is *holy* also to make all people holy and that God's name may be sanctified in them; it is *catholic* furthermore in its openness to diversity that is to be harmonised; and it is likewise *apostolic* because it is also committed to evangelise the whole human person and all people' (EMCC 97).

One important implication of the above is that there is an urgent need for a more effective education that forms in all citizens an appreciation of the global dimension of contemporary societies, economies and cultures and the mutual interdependence of all on this increasingly small planet. Religious education has a particular contribution to make by developing 'a sense of welcome, especially for the poorest and outcasts, as migrants often are. This welcome is fully based on love for Christ, in the certainty that good done out of love of God to one's neighbour, especially the most needy, is done to him' (EMCC 41). Education must also raise awareness of the serious problems that precede and accompany migration, such as the demographic question, work and working conditions (illegal work), the care of the numerous elderly persons, criminality, the exploitation of migrants and the trafficking and smuggling of human beings (cf. EMCC 41).

These themes and issues are further developed by Columban priest, Fr Bobby Gilmore, in his chapter 'The Migrant Heart on a Journey of Hope'. Speaking mainly in the Irish context, Gilmore observes that Ireland, which for so long has been a 'culture of departure', is struggling to develop a 'culture of arrival'. There is a failure to see migration into Ireland in the context of the bigger picture of globalisation, the demands of first world economies, the aging population of Europe and, most importantly, the real risk taken by the migrant as he or she departs and arrives on a journey of hope.

Hospitality and the Earth

Often we regard the migrant as one who is displaced. The displacement of the migrant is an expression of the deeper fact that we are all increasingly displaced from the earth upon whose hospitality our very life depends. This theme is developed by Columban priest, Fr Sean McDonagh, in his chapter 'Abusing this Hospitable Earth'. McDonagh argues that 'care of the earth' and hospitality are intrinsically connected, yet we have been very slow in the Christian Churches to recognise what is happening to the wider earth and to understand that we are guests of the planet. He reflects as a missionary who has witnessed the effects of the egocentricity of the first-third world on the two-thirds world and calls for a critique of the present economic and political structure that is totally destructive of all life (not just human life) and of the very planet upon which all life depends. The exploitation of the economic systems in the two-thirds world is one of the major causes of human migration from these countries to first-third world countries (such as Ireland). The affluence of the few is impoverishing the poor and destroying the earth. One-quarter of the human population live in poverty and this poverty is intrinsically connected to the exploitation of the world's resources. The effects of global warming can be seen in the melting of glaciers, ever more violent storms and rising sea levels. These are not simply natural phenomena; they have human causes, and are further threatening those particularly in the two-thirds world. Our present economic system is destroying the very land, air and water upon which life depends. The survival of all life on this planet demands a global ethic and an ecological conversion that recognises that we are all guests of a hospitable earth.

Hospitality and the Kingdom of God

Hospitality has deep biblical roots and is also at the core of other non-Christian religious expressions. In her chapter, 'Recovering Hospitality as a Christian Tradition', Dr Christine D. Pohl (Professor of Church in Society at Asbury Theological Seminary in Wilmore, Kentucky) argues that hospitality is at the centre of Christian life and discipleship because it is at the centre of the Gospel. She examines the rich resources of the biblical texts of the Old and New Testaments and the historical tradition of the early Christian communities that relate to hospitality. She also charts the decline of hospitality within the Christian community from the fourth century onwards due to its institutionalisation. She highlights the challenge to 'recover hospitality' by seeing those who we welcome not as 'embodied needs' but as persons with unique stories and gifts. The biblical tradition sees hospitality as a strange mixture of very ordinary acts of caring and the promise of God's presence within such acts.

Strangeness and the Stranger in our Midst

The final two chapters of this book explore the intimacy of strangeness. In his chapter, 'Towards a Poetics of Hospitality', Dr John O'Donohue, Irish poet, philosopher and scholar, provocatively explores the implicit philosophy behind the notion of strangeness, the stranger, and the idea of hospitality with a view to grounding a creative and critical poetics of hospitality. He invites us to 'begin a friendship with strangeness that it might become a constant, challenging, creative companion to [our] perception, imagination and feeling'. He defines 'otherness' as 'difference that you cannot immediately domesticate or assimilate'. In answer to the question 'Who is the stranger?', O'Donohue replies, 'Each one of us is the stranger'. We are born as strangers, live in a 'landscape of otherness' and journey towards the incredible strangeness that awaits us at death. Yet we find it difficult to 'make peace' with, and befriend, the stranger inside ourselves. God too is a stranger who invites us to all-embracing intimacy. A phenomenology of 'the stranger' is about the transfiguration of anonymity into intimacy and real presence. Thus, hospitality has a different logic to the functional logic of contemporary society. It is attuned to the logic of the invisible and it gives, not wanting a return. Based upon the philosophy of Levinas, O'Donohue states that the spirituality of the St John of God Order demands something 'subversive and intimate, namely, the image of the human face that resists and, indeed, subverts any institutional claim to appropriate the native integrity of the person'.

In 'Beholding the Stranger in our Midst', Professor John M. Hull (Honorary Professor of Practical Theology in the Queen's Foundation for Ecumenical Theological Education, Birmingham, England) explores the experience of the stranger who is disabled by the reaction of others to the impairment of blindness. Hull notes that, with respect to people who are physically, intellectually or emotionally impaired, a natural conservatism has made the Churches reluctant to discard even those elements of their tradition that are now seriously out of date, both socially and ethically. He argues that people today do not want compassion but the full exercise of their human rights, equality of opportunity and a reasonable level of economic life. The 'pity' often experienced by the disabled from the well-meaning is degrading, and many disabled people experience a 'surplus of compassion' which adds to their estrangement. This flows from a sense of unease on the part of many who, when meeting someone from a different world, may unconsciously seek to protect their own world from challenge by failing to recognise the otherness of the other world. Thus, strangeness is seen as a threat to normality. Hull further notes that one of the most effective techniques of tribalisation is the distinguishing of 'us' from 'them' and that religion can act to initiate and sustain such tribalisation. For the 'stranger' to become the 'welcome guest' we must recognise that we are also strangers who are continually welcomed by God in Christ. We are to live as pilgrims, as exiles, and always be open to those who in some other way are like us, pilgrims, exiles, refugees, or strangers.

Conclusion

In 2000 in Paris, UNESCO promulgated the 'Earth Charter',[2] work on which had been initiated in 1992 at the Earth Summit in Rio de Janeiro. The preamble of the Charter states:

> As the world becomes increasingly interdependent and fragile, the future at once holds great peril and great promise. To move forward we must recognise that in the midst of a magnificent diversity of cultures and life forms we are one human family and one Earth community with a common destiny. We must join together to bring

forth a sustainable global society founded on respect for nature, universal human rights, economic justice and a culture of peace. Towards this end, it is imperative that we, the peoples of Earth, declare our responsibility to one another, to the greater community of life and to future generations.

The preamble goes on to state: 'The spirit of human solidarity and kinship with all life is strengthened when we live with reverence for the mystery of being, gratitude for the gift of life and humility regarding the human place in nature.' These quotations provide a powerful synthesis of the many themes related to 'hospitality as a rule of life' explored in this collection of papers. Achieving such a global ethic requires a change of heart and mind based upon a commitment to ecological integrity, social and economic justice, democracy, non-violence and peace. While the Charter makes no explicit reference to God, it is a profoundly religious, spiritual and ethical document based upon the need for conversion to fundamental transcendent values. Commitment to such values is deepened and enriched by religious faith. Principle 16 of the Charter defines peace as 'the wholeness created by right relationships with oneself, other persons, other cultures, other life, Earth and the larger whole of which all are a part'. It is worth remembering that 'Peace be with you' is the greeting of the risen crucified Christ who was born in a stable, who as an infant fled for his life with his parents as refugees, who during his public life had 'nowhere to lay his head', who shared his table with those regarded as sinners and treated as outcasts, and who was put to death with outcasts outside the gates of the city. May his greeting of 'Peace be with you' be our greeting also to the stranger in our midst.

Notes

1. John Paul II, *Intercultural Integration*, Message for World Day of Migrants and Refugees, Rome: Vatican City, 2005.
2. This is available on-line at http://www.earthcharter.org/files/charter/charter.pdf.

The Jericho Road

Fintan Brennan-Whitmore

When I was a young man preparing to take my vow of hospitality for the first time I was told that the familiar parable of the Good Samaritan was 'the Gospel of Hospitality' and if I wanted to make hospitality 'my special care' I should read it frequently, study it well, know it by heart and take it on as my rule of life. I am not sure that I have succeeded in achieving this last instruction, but having looked at this story from many different angles over many years I am convinced that it contains layers and layers of insight and meaning that can only enrich our understanding of what it is to be hospitable or to behave as a good neighbour towards our fellow human beings. Jesus of Nazareth first told the parable in answer to a lawyer who asked the question that has forever bedevilled us, the deceptively simple question: 'Who is my neighbour?'

Heading for Jericho
This is the story of four people who had one thing in common – they set out from the same place, for the same place, on the same day, although probably at different times. As far as we know they had never met one another before and they came from very different social, economic and political backgrounds, which makes it unlikely that they would ever have wanted to mix with each other in the first place. The road they took was the terribly barren and notoriously difficult highway that stretched from Jerusalem to Jericho. I say notoriously difficult because it had a bad name as a place ruled by rootless bandits who earned their living by mugging hapless travellers, often leaving them half-dead along the side of the road. This is precisely what happened to the first of our four characters. He probably had not got very far into his journey when he fell into the hands of the infamous brigands who, true to form,

left him seriously wounded and unable to move, before they made off with whatever valuables he possessed.

But our story is equally about what happened to the other three characters when they came across the broken body of their fellow traveller on that fateful day. So let us ponder for a while the next two travellers of our foursome, the clergyman and the businessman, as I call them. They both had very similar reactions to what they saw as an obstruction on the road ahead, namely the motionless, bloodstained body of their fellow traveller, whose mugging could only have taken place a short time earlier. Upon seeing what was coming up before them they passed by on the other side of the road. Put in the stark words of this simple narrative this seems a shocking thing to do, to see such dire and obvious human need and to so completely and plainly avoid it. But is not this the reaction, or some variation of it, exactly what we all do to escape having to meet certain people and avoid being caught up in the tangled web of their lives. It is the rare person who has not at some stage found themselves saying, 'Oh my God, will you look at who is coming down the road, I'll pretend I didn't see him, I'll turn the corner here, I hope to God he hasn't seen me, I'll cross over to the other side of the street, I'll run into this shop until he's well past'. We have, of course, very good and plausible reasons for this kind of behaviour – 'I'll will never get where I am are going if I stop to talk'; 'I just can't listen to another terrible story, I'm depressed enough as it is'; 'I don't know what to say in these circumstances'; 'I'm not properly trained for this'.

My own image of this scene in the story is that the two characters could see well what was coming up and decided they didn't want to get caught up in anything that would disturb them, distract them from their day's agenda, or remind them of how vulnerable they were themselves. This is something we all do from time to time. We are afraid that if we see that news item, if we watch that film, if we read that article in the newspaper, if we hear that story from so and so, if we visit that home or encounter them in the street, we will either be too upset that we won't be able to cope, or compelled to get involved in something that we would rather not know about. So, we divert our gaze and go out of our way to avoid encountering anything that will upset us!

The poet, T.S. Eliot, sums this up beautifully in many of his writings, most notably in his play *Murder in the Cathedral* in which the chorus represents the attitude of most towards anything strange, different or upsetting. The chorus keeps insisting that we are living and half-living, that we have our deaths, sicknesses, births, marriages, tragedies and our times of happiness, but that we don't really want anything to happen. Happenings are events which fundamentally change our perspective of life. They draw us away from the familiar and into the world of the strange and the different that we have often spent our lifetime avoiding. Hospitality is the polar opposite of this attitude. It is frequently defined as welcoming the stranger, embracing the different, opening ourselves to the experience that we are not used to, that which does not fit into our ready made, well-worked-out, socio-economic, politico-religious, comfortable understanding of the world and our place in it.

When I read the story of the four characters and their journey down the Jericho road, I imagine that each of them had their own reason for taking the trip. I would also speculate that each person's motivation for being on that trip was just as valid as those of the other three. The first poor fellow didn't have much choice about the direction of his journey; he was never going to continue without the help of others and a considerable amount of rehabilitation. As the story unfolds it is obvious that for the second and the third characters, sticking to their own plans and their own agenda was such an overriding priority that they were prepared to ignore, walk around or over whatever or whoever stood in their way.

The fourth of our characters however had an entirely different attitude. He had no hesitation at all in radically transforming all his plans for the day to help the poor victim he happened upon on the road. Placing a value on hospitality means at the very least being open to changing our priorities to respond to the unexpected human needs of others. Indeed, for people who practise hospitality frequently, or have it high on their list of practical virtues, life will often be what happens to them when they are trying to do something altogether different. Their life story is not what they plan and then manage to achieve, it's about the many interruptions that occur in their lives, which bring them into the strange world of other people and their many concerns and problems.

The problem with hospitality is that it conjures up images of being nice to someone different. The sort of thing that leaves us with cosy feelings of goodness about ourselves and how we have gone out of our way to be helpful to someone else. The Jericho traveller's story as told by Jesus is far from this cosy, good feeling kind of altruism. The Samaritan would have to have done great violence to himself, to his sense of being a Samaritan, to his plans for that particular day, to so many things, for him to be so generous to the person who fell into the hands of the brigands. Firstly, he was a Samaritan, and Jews and Samaritans were sworn enemies of each other. To go out of your way to assist your enemy is to do violence to what is expected of you. But not only does he assist his wounded fellow traveller without the slightest hesitation, the story goes on to describe how he puts him on his own mount, takes him to an inn, ministers to him all night long and the following day pays the inn keeper to continue the care, telling him, 'Whatever expenses you have over and above what I have already paid you, I will make good on my return journey'. What reckless generosity! What an abandonment of normal social interaction! One is left asking, 'Has this guy completely gone over to the cause of the enemy?'; 'Is he trying somehow to make reparation for some terrible past sin?'; 'Has he lost the run of himself?' No, we are told, he is just being a good neighbour, he is just practising hospitality, he is making space in his own schedule, in his own life, in his own wallet for the needs of this total stranger, who should, by all normal reckoning, have been his enemy. Jesus does not build into the story some other possible explanation for the Samaritan's 'over the top' behaviour. This is what it means to be a good neighbour. This and nothing short of it is what hospitality is all about. There really is no way of getting around the violence we have to do to ourselves if we are to respond, even in a small way, to the call of hospitality.

The Jericho and Toledo Roads

The action of the generous Samaritan has many parallels in the life of St John of God. It seems that after his mysterious conversion experience, when he went mad in the streets of Granada, displaying all the characteristics of what we today would call a mental breakdown, John made peace with his God, with himself and with the world. The key element in arriving at this state of peace was his decision to respond to the needs of the poor, the sick and abandoned, no matter what they asked him to do, or where it might take him in life, so long as it did not require him to do anything sinful. It has been said that John's behaviour during this part of his life was consistent with someone who made a pact, or took a private vow that he was going to allow the course of the rest of his life be directed by the dire human needs of the people around him. He partially explained this when he said: 'If I am being fooled, that is their concern. All I know is that I do what I am doing for the love of God.'

One example of John's reckless generosity, which has features similar to those found in the Jericho Road story, is the account of a certain trip that John made to Toledo. Here John completely accepted, without any questions or expressions of doubt, the tale of four prostitutes who promise him that they will reform their lives if he first agrees to take them to Toledo! John set out with his faithful companion Angulo to take them on this lengthy and expensive journey, completely accepting their word. Angulo constantly questioned the folly of the whole thing. The people they met on the road sneered and shouted coarse remarks at these two men accompanied by four women, whose dress and demeanour could not be described as modest. When Angulo exploded in anger at the attitude of the women, their behaviour along the way and the fact that three of them took off in the middle of the journey itself, John either said nothing, called for more patience, or reminded Angulo that at least one of the women remained faithful to her word. Impressed by John's respect and disinterested, positive regard for her, something which she had never seen in a man before, this last woman eventually began to believe in herself and in time was able to completely change her life. John's conclusion about the whole thing could be summed up by saying, 'wasn't that really worth it!'

We cannot claim to take hospitality seriously, nor can we claim to have embraced the Jericho Road story as Jesus tells it unless, at least once in our lives, we make a Toledo Journey. To consider making such a journey, it is useful and maybe even necessary to believe in your heart of hearts that responding to the basic human needs of our fellow human beings should take precedence over all other considerations. Taking a Toledo Journey with someone means taking a risk with him or her, trusting way beyond what the regular, socio-economic, ethnic or political boundaries expect of us. What is important about taking a Toledo Journey is our motivation for making the journey in the first place. To be authentic it has to be a faith journey. Scripture tells us that God so loved the world that he sent his only son to join the human family, to be as we are. We believe that this was God's great plan for our salvation, God's Toledo Journey, entrusting his son to the human experience. What an enormous thing it is to believe in a God who puts so much trust in us when we so rarely display any trust in one another. The vicious, cruel, blood-thirsty history of humanity makes us most unworthy of a God who (in another of the many rich images given to us by Jesus) comes rushing out to meet us while we are still a long way off. To be a Christian is to believe that God loves us humans that much. It surely follows then that to act in a Christian way, to be a neighbour as the Gospel puts it, our behaviour should reflect or imitate the reckless generosity of our God.

The synoptic Gospels sum up the preaching of Jesus in one short sentence: 'The Kingdom of God is at hand; Repent.' The first phrase of the statement describes what is happening in the incarnation and the ministry of Jesus. The one-word second phrase tells us what we are supposed to do about it. The history of Christianity is littered with the dead and wounded bodies of believers who slaughtered one another because they disagreed about the meaning of that second phrase. They had different versions about what they were supposed to do now that they were Christians! So, the word 'repent' has proved difficult to translate, to say the least. It can mean 'ask for forgiveness', 'radically change your heart', or 'stop and turn around'. Whatever disputes there might be among Christians, one thing that all traditions agree on is that once you have embraced Christ, you can't be 'business as usual'. You can't park your faith in a certain corner of your life alongside the other things that interest or amuse you. As Jesus himself put it, you don't put the new wine of his Good News into the old skins of our lives. No, the new wine requires new skin, a transformation of our life, a whole, different outlook.

The call of the Jericho Road story is not that we conduct our business as usual or that we make minor alterations because of some interruptions that happen on the journey. On the contrary, the call of Jericho is that, in response to human need, we take a different road altogether. In other words, that we allow the human needs of others to shape the course of our journey. Maybe what we are being called to understand in this story is that the things which disrupt, change or alter the plans we have made for ourselves are the very things that the Lord has been inviting us to in life!

What Awaits us at the End of the Road?

It seems that one of the questions that was always being put to Jesus was, 'What are things like on the other side?; How are things organised?' We even have the spectacle of a mother coming right out with it and asking him directly if he would fix it so that her sons would have the best places when they come into his kingdom. Jesus does not answer any of these questions directly, except to remind us that we should not be worried about such things. 'Hasn't God counted every hair on our head!', he tells us and he reminds us that the Father 'has prepared many rooms in his house' for us! Matthew 25 does give us a further glimpse into what is important about the hereafter. Here, Jesus speaks of a time when the Son of Man will come 'in all his glory' and all the peoples of the world will be gathered before him. We can just imagine the scene: it's the end of the world as we know it, everything is over and done with and the reckoning is about to take place. We can see all those individual people, including ourselves, filled with fear perhaps but definitely wondering how we are going to justify our lives.

We are all preoccupied with questions such as, 'What kind of person was I in the first place?'; 'What good did I really do?' Remembering various happenings and specific incidents, we might very well be in a sweat, pondering whether we have a really good excuse for this or that or whether we can point the blame in a different direction! Then, as in so many other gospel texts, the Lord brings into this 'Divine Comedy' his great element of surprise, so that even the most righteous amongst us is left stunned and amazed. For, according to this parable of Jesus, it is not any of the things that we regard as our achievements (be they imagined or real, great or small) that will win us the golden crown! In fact, it seems that none of the many things that we constantly use to justify, excuse or explain our lives really count when all is said and done. According to the Lord himself, it was the cup of water given, the clothes donated on that particular day, the stranger welcomed, or the sick or imprisoned person visited, that will save us in the end. The 'sting in the tail' of this eschatological parable is that even the most righteous among us is unable to remember when they did any of these things. This is presumably because in the normal course of the evaluation of our lives we rarely if ever rate on the scale of our achievements the things which Jesus so clearly prioritises in his Gospels.

The story of our redemption begins with the incarnation: God so loving the world that he sent his only son to be as we are. In other words, he created within the divine space room where we humans can enjoy the fullness of all that we are called to be. This fullness is something which, as Paul points out, we can only now see dimly and occasionally as through a first-century mirror. It surely follows then that we best glimpse the mirror image of that fullness in our own flawed humanity when we repeat God's redemptive action in our own lives. When we create a free and empty space within the murky reality of our own confused lives for another human being who is different, alien or challenging for us, or as is the case with our Samaritan traveller, someone who in the normal course of events should have been our sworn enemy, hospitality then is at the very heart of our response to the Good News that the Kingdom of God is at hand!

Conclusion

If the story of the Jericho road is, as I perceive it to be, a metaphor for the journey of life itself, then we have to radically rethink our goals. Maybe at the end of the day it is not all about getting where we want to go, achieving what we have set out for ourselves. Success may not in fact be about you or me arriving at our Jericho, safe, uninterrupted, the first to arrive. Maybe it is about all of us getting there together, and the only way that we are going to achieve this is if we can lean on, hold up and support one another, so that we all enjoy the fullness of a life complete. Viewed in this way, our arrival at 'Jericho' may not be as fast-tracked and spectacular as we expected. If individual achievement and being more able-bodied than most others is what we think it's all about, we are going to be hugely disappointed when we hear for ourselves that 'the last shall be first and the first shall be last'. We shall be judged according to the hospitality we have lived.

The Migrant Heart on a Journey of Hope

Bobby Gilmore

A Culture of Departure, not of Arrival

When Galway football or hurling teams travel to Dublin I am requested to act as their chaplain. On All Ireland day, September 2001, having fulfilled my chaplaincy obligations, I returned to play golf at Royal Tara Golf Club in Co. Meath. As it happened, Galway's opponents were Meath. A large group of football enthusiasts, having finished their golf early, were sitting around discussing the upcoming afternoon's event. Meath supporters were in no doubt that their team would succeed and send Galway supporters home 'in mourning'. Galway supporters, and others in the group, derided Meath aficionados with all kinds of banter.

However, one piece of banter struck and bothered me. One of the outsiders, trying to puncture the Meath man's confidence, remarked, 'Ah sure, most of the Meath team are *builte isteach* (blow-ins) anyway'. A Meath native challenged this charge, to which the outsider responded, 'Sure didn't their grandparents come here from Galway and Mayo in 1926'. The banter continued, but the *builte isteach* retort intrigued me. I wondered why, after almost eighty years, the descendants of internal migrants were still seen as 'outsiders'. I kept asking myself, 'how long does it take to become an "insider"?' Of course, the resistance to immigrants I was finding in talks with students and adult groups around Ireland had sharpened my antennas. I wondered how Ireland, with three million of its citizens living abroad, of which more than a million are Irish nationals, could be anti-immigrant and, in instances, racist. I wondered why I was hearing the same myths directed against immigrants in Ireland that Irish emigrants had experienced abroad over the centuries – the charges of being 'lazy, dirty, on welfare, ripping-off the system'. It seemed that little has been ascertained and understood, (for instance, that asylum seekers are not allowed to work). Also, those who try to explain that the vast majority of foreigners in Ireland are working in the economy, paying taxes and contributing to society, had similarly not been heard. It seemed that the predictable, sensationalist, anti-immigrant views of the tabloid press held sway in the conversation.

A few weeks later, I was giving talks on migration in Midleton, Co. Cork. Having a few hours to spare I visited Cobh, the port from which Irish emigrants set off on their journeys around the world. The local tourist brochure highlighted the fact that Cobh had been the last port of call for the Titanic. But it also gave prominence to the Immigration Museum. Entering the museum I was greeted with a notice on the wall stating that 'More than three million people left Ireland through this port'. Apart from the shock of the numbers involved, this answered my confusion about the *builte isteach* incident in the golf club.

My conclusion is that Ireland has a culture of departure and, while tourists are acceptable, Ireland is awkward with 'arrivals', those coming to stay. We label such 'people of arrival' with many names: 'asylum seekers', 'refugees', 'migrant workers' or 'immigrants'. Not only are these labels new, but so also are the faces, the clothes and the languages. Inadequate information has been publicly disseminated to explain the arrival of strangers and the factors that have brought them to Ireland. Conversely, little had been done over the years to understand our own Irish emigration, its causes at home and its impact abroad. It was only in the late 1990s that Irish emigration began to be officially recognised in terms of the loss to the 'energy sector' of the population in Irish life, the contribution that Irish emigrants made in the form of remittances to the Irish State and the impact of Irish emigrants in the societies where they settled.

Ireland today has an urban mindset. Over the past forty years there has been a significant shift in the population towards old towns, new towns and the edges of cities. I get the impression visiting schools in new urban areas that people are strangers to themselves. The arrival of those who are different and strange adds to the dislocation already felt. There are few visible soul-warming signs and symbols that are familiar for either the 'local' or the 'foreigner'. And in this scenario, if the 'arrival' is not facilitated, the weak and the immigrant will become scapegoats for the tensions being experienced in change, loss and re-invention. Racist language and activity is frequently experienced as locals try to relocate their own identity.

The Representation of the Immigrant

The use of the 'immigration card' in all recent European election campaigns is not helping the integration and adjustment of migrants. Why consign a debate on immigration to the heat of a local, national or European election? A newspaper heading in the 2005 British General Election ran: 'It's the race issue, stupid. If Labour wants to shake people out of their apathy it simply cannot ignore immigration and asylum.'[1] However, there is some progress to be seen thanks to the emergence of moderating voluntary agencies that are enabling the various cultures to meet each other in respect rather than in strife.

It is difficult to assess and understand why there is such a negative institutional attitude towards immigration in the main trading blocks of the European Union, the North American Free Trade Area and the Asian Basin. All demographic reports indicate that all these economies need immigrants. Historically, it seems that modern industrial nations, in building identities, have drawn on the dualities which oppose 'civilisation' and 'barbarism', 'development' and 'underdevelopment', 'north' and 'south' or 'like' and 'dislike'. Is this because the institutions are more in tune with the anxieties of Buchanan, Huntington, Debray, Le Pen and others, rather than with objective demographic research? As a result, the immigrant is seen as a risk to a way of life and to culture, and as a source of the fragmentation of society. And this is happening at a time of increased awareness of globalisation through mass travel and communication:

> When people are more inclined to use travel as a way to affirm their connection with humanity, to measure the things we have in common ... [travel] is less about being jolted out of your own world than about feeling bolted to a wider one ... [and becoming]

a global citizen. ... Rather than feeling an outsider looking in, the global citizen is at home wherever s/he goes, and feels as connected to and responsible for any Himalayan village, Amazonian rain forest, or African desert on the itinerary, as s/he does to his/her hometown.[2]

Our economies need the talent and resources that migrants bring. For instance, research indicates that in the European Union there are less than two people between the ages of sixteen and sixty-four for every person over the age of sixty-four. The business sections of newspapers are regularly asking whose taxes will pay for health, for education, for welfare or for pensions? Yet, instead of looking at 'managed migration' all we hear about is 'immigration control'. So, do we send Granny to Manila, or do we have a managed immigration policy that enhances the immigrant's decision to risk leaving home and undertake a 'journey of hope'?

Like it or not, in the contemporary phase of globalisation there are new perceptions of 'home' and of 'away'. Recently, Peter van der Veer of the University of Amsterdam wrote that the post-colonial cities of today show a massive deprovincialisation of the world, or a new cosmopolitanism.[3] Another writer, Clifford Geertz, expresses these sentiments:

As the entanglements of everybody with everybody else have grown in recent times to the point where everybody is tripping over everyone's feet and everybody is in everyone's face, its disruptive power, its capacity to induce doubts in those who think they have things figured out, taped, under control, rapidly increases. We live in a bazaar, not a cathedral, a whirl, not a diagram, and this makes it difficult for anyone anymore to be wholly at ease with his or her own ideas, no matter how official, no matter how cherished, no matter how plated with certainty.[4]

Ultimately, immigration implies leaving home. The immigrant, in leaving home, leaves the comfort of the familiar and enters a liminal period of discomfort in unfamiliar surroundings. Even with the demise of distance, immigration is, and always will be, a psychological journey, a journey of hope. Migration is not an act of God; it is caused, and the causes today are no different from those of the past – poverty, debt, trade and tariff regulations, or political corruption. Poverty is the absence of choice. The television screen in the local village shows a better life elsewhere. The mirage of the tourist advert is not confined to the affluent suburbs of the United States, Japan or the European Union. Anyway, the immigrant's national wealth has already preceded them to stock exchanges and investment banks in immigrant destinations in a manner similar to what happened in Ireland in the 1970s, 80s and 90s.

Immigrants risk their lives by going into exile because in many instances they see themselves as half-exiles at home. Ireland needs 40,000 immigrants annually to do the '3D' jobs in the mother-care sector, in health, the care of the elderly, in the service industry, in construction, agribusiness and tourism. Immigrants contribute to economies both 'away' by their work and 'at home' by their remittances. They are the best agents of international development. In 2004, immigrant remittances globally were $126 billion; international Government Aid was $64 billion.

Understanding the Migrant Heart on a Journey of Hope

To understand the immigrant we must develop an understanding of the migrant heart trying to cope with loneliness, meaningless and marginalisation. Irish people cannot avoid, even if they tried, understanding the loneliness of migration. The grief expressed in our songs and stories is no different for contemporary immigrants as it was for Irish emigrants. But loneliness is more than not having friends. It is the permanent cracked feeling of being unhinged from primary relationships, the source of belonging, love and sustenance. All immigrants take risks, but these pale in significance when they talk about loneliness. It is the deepest aspiration of all migrants to participate fully in the social, economic and political life of the communities in which they seek to make their new home.

Meaninglessness in the migrant's life arises from doing menial, dangerous and difficult jobs and the resultant gap between who they are and what they do. Migrants work longer hours but they often see that locals are paid more for doing the same work. Many have to negotiate a day's work and wages on a city kerb. One immigrant remarked to me recently, 'My life is a constant struggle; all I know is worry. But I know God is with me'.

Marginalisation has many sources in the migrant's life. It arises from negative media headlines, racist remarks and political debates about controlling immigration (as if to migrate was a conspiracy and immigrants were to be regarded as vermin). Being made to feel marginal comes from being regarded as suspect, being rejected, degraded and invisible in the networks of life. Recent media research in Ireland indicated that sixty-six per cent of Irish people still have no contact with non-nationals. According to Danial Groody, Mexican immigrants in the United States of America report that 'we are constantly reminded that we are inferior to everybody else and not worth as much as others in American society. And sometimes we wonder if that is how God feels too'.[5] Remarks by people in Irish public life sends a similar message to migrant workers in Ireland.

Is this hope in the migrant's heart a symbol of anything for the Irish memory or imagination? Does the fragility of the migrant, and his or her experience of isolation, dislocation and separateness not remind us of anything? It seems to me that the immigrant in Ireland is the linchpin that reminds us of our own vulnerable, creative migrant history and of the vibrancy and fragility of our future.

The Christian Response

So, what should the Christian response be? To roll-up, hedgehog-like, become anonymous, culturally bleached in indifference and non-interference, to see people as files, post-codes or reference numbers, or just as objects of national security and consumerism rather than as subjects of their own destiny interacting with others in community? There are of course a number of obvious things that can be done. At a personal level an attitude of watchfulness and awareness is needed; for instance, it is important to be mindful of our language. Racist language and remarks are uncouth, uncivil and vulgar. Racism is de-creative; it destroys a person's confidence. It is not just the few racist bigots who are present in all societies that are hurtful. More damaging is the spineless silence of bystanders when racist remarks are voiced. If our friends or associates are racist, we need to tell them the truth. Further, Christians, as individuals and as communities, should campaign for immigration policies that are comparable to trade and capital transfer procedures.

For Ireland and the European Union, a mental decolonisation that will challenge us to assume the plight of others as our own must happen, with all the commitments and responsibilities which this entails. The horrible history of twentieth-century Europe in its treatment of diversity and difference cannot be unlived, but it needn't be repeated. As Holocaust survivor, Elie Weisel, puts it:

> If foreigners frighten me,
> It is because they resemble me in some way.
> They frighten me because, ultimately, I am afraid of myself.
> And what if these people were me?
> The truth is that they are.
> Or, rather,
> It behoves me to act as if they were.
> If he or she is a foreigner in my country,
> Then I will be one too.

Thus, we are constantly challenged to imagine creative responses that see difference other than as a deficit. If we don't, then history and the maintenance of the status quo will succeed. According to the Archbishop of Canterbury, Rowan Williams, the authentic Christian community must always be asking, 'who is being excluded?'

Conclusion: ' ... and You Welcomed Me'

The Christian should be aware of biblical and Church teaching in relation to the stranger. Jesus identified himself with the stranger and his parents were migrants. We should always remember that the God who loves only us does not exist. Neither does the God exist who expects us to love only those who love us. The desire of everybody, including the immigrant, is to feel 'at home'. Gary Younge, writing in *The Guardian*, captures this well:

> Until I was seventeen, whenever people asked where I was from, I would tell them Barbados, the land of my parents, despite the fact that I had made one visit at the age of four. I meant it. Sadly, it had little meaning. It took a trip to Barbados to realise that they had little interest in me as a citizen either. Between them, racism and migration had ensured that my longing for a sense of belonging would, in all likelihood, not be satisfied by geography. Over the years I would discover that home was where I felt at home, it was about my values, not my postcode.[6]

Robert Frost puts it more succinctly in his poem, *The Death of a Hired Man*:

> Home is a place where, when you have to go there,
> They have to take you in.
> I should have called it
> Something you somehow haven't to deserve.[7]

For the Christian, these quotations are strongly reminiscent of the father who, in the parable of the Lost Son, rushes down along the road to welcome home his estranged younger son returning, penniless, from a distant land. The son falls at the father's feet but the father lifts him up, presses him to his heart, joyously celebrates his presence and shares everything he has with him. The Christian is called to such watchfulness, welcome and generosity:

Lifting others, we ourselves are lifted.
Happiness – the sense of a life well lived –
Is born in the blessings we bestow on others.
Bringing to someone else's life
Brings meaning to our own.[8]

Notes

1. *The Times* (London), 4 April 2005.
2. *Newsweek,* 11 April 2004.
3. P. Van der Veer, 2001, *Transnational Religion,* Paper given at a Conference on Transnational Migration, Comparative Perspectives, Princetown University, 30 June – 1 July 2001.
4. C. Geertz, quoted by Van der Veer.
5. Cf. D. Groody, *Border of Death, Valley of Life: An Immigrant Journey of Heart and Spirit,* Lanham MD: Rowman and Littlefield Publishers, Inc., 2002.
6. G. Younge, 'Home is not a Postcode', *The Guardian.* 7 February 2005.
7. R. Frost, 1915, *The Death of a Hired Man,* http://www.bartleby.com /118/3.html.
8. Rabbi Jonathan Sacks, *The Times,* 11 June 2005.

Abusing this Hospitable Earth

Sean McDonagh

Introduction

'Care of the earth' and hospitality are intrinsically connected, yet we have been very slow in the Christian Churches to understand that we are guests of the planet and to recognise what is happening to the wider earth. Our analysis must therefore include not just how our policies are affecting humankind, but how we are affecting the systems on which we depend – the air, the water and the soils that sustain us within the web of life. This is a spiritual, religious and moral challenge that must be addressed in a substantive and effective way. Let me start with a parable that captures some aspects of the present ecological crisis. It is based upon an insight I came across in the writings of the Muslim scholar Fazlun Khalid.[1]

In medieval times a group of nobility were invited to a banquet in a castle. The food was so sumptuous and the drink so delicious that they simply could not get enough. They continued to gorge themselves long after the point of satiation. As the night wore on, instead of ending the meal, relaxing and going home, the revellers became more and more intent on securing additional helpings of the mouth-watering food. Eventually the food started to run out. The Lord and Lady of the castle did not want to lose face before their guests. They sent out their militia to the local farms to seize what they could; rice, corn, the odd pig, whatever. And so the cooking and feasting continued. But then the firewood to cook the banquet started to run out and getting more wood became a problem, and then the supply of wood completely ran out. One of the guests said, 'Look at all these wonderful timber pillars in this banqueting hall; if we just take little slivers of the pillars we can continue to cook the food'. The other guests agreed. Hatchets and knives were brought, the pillars were cut, the kitchen fire was stoked, and the food for the banquet continued to be cooked. After a while cracks began to appear in the ceiling. But the banqueters were so distracted that they were completely oblivious to what was happening. They simply didn't give a thought to the fact that unless they stopped hacking at the supporting pillars the ceiling would eventually come crashing down on their heads. Their obsession with food was endangering not only those who were feasting but everyone else in the castle compound.

The din, buzz and activity in the banqueting hall and the kitchen was electrifying. People were milling around the cooking stoves, shouting orders for more food and eating with relish. Yet not everyone was caught up in the frenzy. A small number of onlookers stood by the doors with neither plates nor glasses in their hands. They implored the revellers to end their meal and avert the disaster that was threatening. A few of those eating would occasionally stop to listen to their heartfelt pleas. They did begin to murmur, 'Our meal is on the backs of the poor; we have taken what other people need to keep alive, their very sustenance'. One or two noticed the cracks beginning to appear on the ceiling and thought to themselves, 'Someday soon we should get that roof checked or it might collapse'. But as soon as a waiter with food came close they would lose interest and join in the scramble for more. The majority of those who were celebrating however were too engrossed in their meal to pay any attention at all. Nothing else mattered but their banquet.

Where do we find ourselves in the parable? With the banqueting nobles? With those outside the banqueting hall whose food was seized? With those who were aware of the injustice to the poor or with those who protested about the damage to the banqueting hall but who still continued to feast? Perhaps those who protested about the injustice to the poor can be identified with the Church groups – people like members of the Society of St Vincent de Paul or various development organisations that have a Christian background. Perhaps we can identify with Friends of the Earth or Greenpeace, who also tried to point out the irreparable damage to the very place in which hospitality was being enjoyed. And what of the minority of the revellers who engaged with both protesting groups. What did they say to the 'justice-minded protestors'? Did they say: 'We deserve this banquet, we have created this wealth and we are really fed up of your "bleeding hearts" critique. Really, get with it and come in and join the party.' And what did they say to environmentally-minded protestors? Did they say: 'The problems with the ceiling are minor. There is a little bit of a sag, but tomorrow morning we will have our engineers in. Our technologies will solve that little problem. Don't be worrying about this thing falling apart; it's not going to happen.' And what of the other nobles and the buzz in the banqueting hall? Our modern industrial economy is so attractive and energetic and seems to be working so effectively and efficiently that most people are completely engrossed in it. They have a mortgage, they want to give education to their children, they are looking forward to a vacation – they are so engrossed they fail to notice the deteriorating state of the very planet that is offering them hospitality.

For me the parable highlights the fact that we are causing extensive and often irreversible damage to our air, our water and our companion species. I reflect not primarily as an ecologist, nor as a development worker, although I have been extensively involved in a variety of roles in the ecological and development arena. I reflect as a missionary, as one who has witnessed the effects of the egocentricity of the first-third world on the two-thirds world. Of course we must welcome the stranger in our midst and offer hospitality to the migrant. However, we need to situate our concerns and our critique within the economic and political structure that is totally destructive of all life (not just human life) and of the very planet upon which all life depends.

Option for the Poor
Today there are 1.5 billion people, that is one-fourth of the population of the world, who are living in absolute poverty. This is a challenge to the conscience of us all, not just missionaries. All Christians today are challenged by the tenets of our Churches to promote justice and to

make a preferential option for those who are poor, discriminated against or marginalised by a particular religious, social, cultural or economic system. For some communities in the two-thirds 'developing world' this still means providing education, health care or emergency relief for those who are forgotten by society or, like so many in Africa today, facing death by starvation. But we must also ask why poverty is so widespread and prevalent, and, sadly, is actually increasing in the world today, after four decades of so-called 'development'. We must insistently ask why so many people are poor, why so many are forced to leave their native lands and, as economic migrants, become strangers in another land? And we must not be content with facile answers from the corporate media or from those who idolise the market and its workings. As a missionary, it was my privilege to work among the poor and to see in the faces of individuals and communities how the destructive global economy really works.

In the final months of his life, addressing the Diplomatic Corps accredited to the Holy See on 10 January 2005, the late Pope John Paul II called for a moral mobilisation in the face of the dramatic problem of starvation in our world. He noted the contradiction that our world has been made wondrously fruitful by its creator and yet hundreds of millions of human beings are suffering from grave malnutrition and each year millions of children die of hunger or its effects. He went on to call for a radical commitment to justice and for a more attentive and determined display of solidarity. Such a radical commitment to justice, I believe, must begin to seriously challenge the idolatry of the market and the present economic system that is destroying individuals, communities and the earth itself.

Affluence is Impoverishing the Poor and Destroying the Earth

In many of my writings, especially *Passion for the Earth* (1994), I try to show that the demands made by our modern affluent way of living are impoverishing whole populations, especially in the two-thirds world. Any economic and political system that creates such gross inequalities stands condemned by the Gospel of Jesus. The constant teaching of the Hebrew and Christian Scriptures, and of all the Christian

Churches, is that the goods of this world are meant to sustain all human life on earth.

This same system is 'killing' the earth itself. I consider this point in greater detail in my books – *To Care for the Earth* (1986), *The Greening of the Church* (1990), *Passion for the Earth* (1994), *Greening the Christian Millennium* (1999), *Why are we Deaf to the Cry of the Earth?* (2001), *Patenting Life? Stop: Is Corporate Greed Forcing us to Eat Genetically Engineered food?* (2003), *Dying for Water* (2003) and *The Death of Life: The Horror of Extinction* (2004). In these I argue that our current economic system is precipitating extensive changes to the biosphere and is diminishing life on earth for all future generations of humans and of other creatures. This devastation of the earth is contrary to the teaching of Jesus who proclaimed: 'I have come that they may have life and have it to the full' (Jn 10:10).

Impoverishing the Poor through the Transfer of Wealth

Our modern, industrial, throw-away society has benefited multinational corporations, the rich and the middle class in the first-world and indeed the elite in the two-thirds world, but it has further impoverished the poor. Third world debt is an example of a mechanism that enables rich countries to fleece the two-thirds world countries. The debts were contracted with the connivance of northern governments and bankers in the 1970s when northern banks were flush with petrodollars, wished to recycle them, and in the process make a hefty profit. These northern governments knew that the loans were being made to repressive regimes such as the Marcos regime in the Philippines, which, it is commonly believed, embezzled much of the money and squandered the rest on projects which were of little benefit to the majority of poor people in the country. In the early 1980s the debts ballooned out of control, mainly through currency fluctuations, rising interest rates and the dramatic drop in commodity prices in northern countries. Serving these debts is placing an enormous burden on most southern countries today.

Many of us believe we are helping the two-thirds world. For instance, in 2005 eighteen of the poorest nations of the world were informed by the G8 Summit that their debts were going to be cancelled and US$33 billion was to be made available. That is a pittance in comparison to what the developed west receives from these countries. Let me illustrate how much we have benefited. Susan George, a political economist, in her book *The Debt Boomerang* (1992) provides the figures involved in this transfer of wealth to the rich. During the period 1982 to 1990 there was a net transfer of $418 billion from the poor south to the rich north through debt repayments alone. To give some idea of the huge sums involved she calculates that the poor of the world have financed six Marshall Plans for the rich through the single mechanism of debt servicing alone. (The Marshall Plan was that United States initiative to rebuild Europe and Japan after the Second World War, partly for altruistic reasons, and partly to grow the US economy by providing a market for its goods.)

Today the World Bank and the International Monetary Fund (IMF) are imposing conditions of repayment on the two-thirds world through Structural Adjustment Programmes (SAPs) which are leading to starvation, illiteracy, political and social breakdown and the irreversible destruction of important ecosystems such as the rainforests. The suffering entailed in this was summed up seventeen years ago in a 1989 UNICEF report as follows: 'Hundreds of thousands of the developing world's children have given their lives to pay their countries' debts, and many millions more are still paying the interest with their malnourished minds and bodies.'[2] There is very little public awareness that institutions such as the International Monetary Fund and the World Bank have acted as conduits for transferring the produce, the labour and the work of third world peoples to support the economies of the west and have left the kinds of devastation that we see today in countries like the Philippines.

The present economic system benefits about 1.3 billion people, mainly in first-third countries such as North America, Europe, Australia, and of course the elite in the two-thirds world countries. There are about four billion other people on this planet that do not benefit from the present economic system. One should be careful not to over-generalise, but there is no way that the 6.6 billion people who live on planet earth could live in the affluent way that we live. This would take about three or four planets like planet earth and, as far as we know from astronomers, there is no other such place within twenty or thirty or forty million light years. So it can't be done. This is the central issue of justice at the heart of all development aid and it challenges the way we live and the way we use the earth's resources.

Destroying the Earth

Once one begins to present the statistics relating to the destruction of the earth, people's ears begin to close as they feel overwhelmed. Thus, the most important thing to do when looking at the details of environmental devastation is to present it in an adequate context so that the implications of the data can be appreciated. One of the problems with environmental issues is that we often present them one after another as a 'litany'. This trivialises the environmental issue for two reasons. Firstly, each new report of environmental damage is seen in isolation and thus the cumulative and global impact of what is happening can easily be missed. Looked at merely on a case-by-case basis we can delude ourselves into thinking that ecological destruction is not a serious threat to life and that environmental campaigners are like the boy who cried 'Wolf', simply trying to attract attention when there is no real danger. Secondly, there is often a time-lag problem. No sane person will jump from a five-storey building and expect to survive; the result of such an action is immediate. But this is not the case for environmental problems such as global warming, acid rain, ozone depletion or mercury poisoning. It may take decades before the impact of our present actions becomes apparent or their effect on human communities fully appreciated. Since our industrial society is focused on immediate responses and short-term gratification this time-lag permits politicians and communities to push environmental issues to one side and concentrate instead on tangible immediate problems such as unemployment or inflation.

Much is at stake; the scale of the destruction is enormous. Not only are we contributing to human pain and injustice, we are also destroying our air, water, sunlight and soils. We are causing the extinction of a vast number of creatures that God has placed on this earth with us. Every part of the globe and every ecosystem on earth is now affected, in some situations in an irreversible way. The cumulative effect is that we are bringing about changes of a geological and even cosmic order of magnitude. Nothing similar to it has ever happened in the history of humankind or at least in the 12,000 years since humans first became farmers. The human, moral and religious challenge of our times is to halt this destruction and heal, where possible, the damage that has already been inflicted on the planet.

The most comprehensive way of understanding our present situation is to see it from a geological and biological perspective rather than a historical or cultural perspective. The changes which humans have brought about to the planet in the past two hundred years (especially in the last fifty years) are changing the chemistry of the air and water, transforming the soils and effecting a 'mega-extinction'. In a very real sense we are witnessing the end of an age, the Cenozoic era, which has lasted for the past sixty million years and during which most of the life forms with which we are familiar came to full flowering. Today we are challenged to enter what one commentator, Thomas Berry, names the 'Ecozoic period' or the 'ecological age'. This will require a new sensitivity towards all living and non-living members of the natural community to which we belong. As we will see later, this will mean a major shift from our present exclusively 'human-centred' religious and moral preoccupation to an eco-centred one. But first we consider how crucial life systems on our planet have already been damaged.

Global Warming

Consider global warming. We are changing the chemistry of the air. The atmospheric concentration of carbon dioxide, methane, chlorofluorocarbons (CFCs) and other 'greenhouse' gases are expected to increase by 30% in coming decades. This build-up is likely to increase the earth's surface temperature by between 1.5 and 4.5 degrees centigrade by the year 2030. A study by a group of scientists in preparation for the international meeting on global warming in The Hague in November 2000 suggested that the 'upper range of warming over the next hundred years could be far higher than was estimated in 1995'.[3] Global warming will cause major, and in the main, deleterious climatic changes. In northern latitudes winters will probably be shorter and wetter. Sub-tropical areas might become drier and more arid, and tropical ones wetter. The changes will have major, but as yet unpredictable, effects on agriculture and natural ecosystems.

Melting Ice

As the oceans warm up and expand, sea levels will rise, leading to severe flooding over lowland areas. In March 2002 scientists in the Antarctica revealed that the Larsen B ice shelf had disappeared from the map, setting 500 million billion tonnes of water afloat. Glaciologists were taken aback by the speed with which the area disintegrated; it took only thirty-one days. This disintegration has dumped more ice into the southern ocean than all the icebergs for the past fifty years. The reason for this rapid disintegration is the rise in temperature by 2.5 degrees Celsius in the past fifty years. This will particularly affect the very people who had nothing to do with causing global warming in the first place; people living in two-thirds countries. For example, a rise of a metre and a half in sea levels would wipe out much of lowland Bangladesh, adding 'ecological migrants' to the existing 'economic migrants'. Other low-lying areas of countries such as Egypt could simply disappear, also creating enormous migration problems. Even first-world cities like Venice are feeling the effects of global warming as the sea rises around it.

Melting glaciers are also creating potential disasters. There are about 160,000 glaciers on earth. Only about forty of these have been monitored closely. During the past twenty years many of these are melting. In the next five years it is predicted that as many as forty lakes that have been formed by melting ice high up in the Himalayas, especially in Nepal and Bhutan, could burst their banks and cause devastation in lowland valleys. According to Paul Brown (2002) there are 'thought to be hundreds more such liquid time-bombs in India, Pakistan, Afghanistan, Tibet and China'.[4] This situation is rendered more dangerous by the fact that many of these lakes are in geologically active areas. A sizeable earthquake could trigger a disaster. If the Himalayan glaciers melt they will drain into the rivers Indus, Ganges, Brahmaputra, Mekong and Yangtze. One-third of the world's population live in the vicinity of these rivers and if the volume of the water they transmit increases dramatically the effects on agriculture and thus on humanity will be catastrophic. A recent conference organised by the Pontifical Academy of Sciences and the United Nations ambassador to the Holy See was entitled 'Feeding a Hungry World – the Moral Imperative of Biotechnology'. Today there is an increasing emphasis on the supposed need to have genetically engineered foods in order to adequately feed the world. But the major problem facing agriculture in the next three decades is in fact global warming. Many of the countries that are promoting genetically modified food have not signed up to the Kyoto Protocol on climate change. The negative impact of climate change on agricultural production is considerably greater than the predicted positive impact of biotechnology.

More Frequent and increasingly Violent storms

It is probable that as a result of climate change storms of great ferocity will become more frequent. When Hurricane Mitch slammed into Central America in October 1998 the devastating floods and mudslides killed over 10,000 people on the Caribbean coast of Venezuela. The storms that battered France immediately after Christmas in 1999 caused thirty-seven deaths and had an estimated direct cost of $16 billion.[5] In 2004 and 2005 hurricanes again tore through the Caribbean and into the southern United States, causing numerous deaths and massive damage to property. According to Sir David King, a chief scientist with the British government, climate change is the most serious issue that has faced the planet for 5,000 years. So far our political, economic and religious institutions have not faced up to this reality. In our Catholic tradition we have sustained reflection on issues such as contraception and abortion but the reality of climate change could threaten the life of tens of millions of people in countries like the Philippines and Bangladesh, and in many of the major low-lying cities of the world. A rise of one metre in Manila for example would cover most of metro Manila, which houses about eight million people. Surely these issues too relate to our concerns with the sacredness of life?

Effects on the Climate of Britain and Ireland

A joint report sponsored by the British government and climate change scientists was released in April 2002. The report stated that the planet was warmer in the first three months of 2002 than at any time in the previous one thousand years. The report predicts that the weather in Britain and Ireland will become warmer and more unstable. This trend has continued: 2004 was the second warmest year on record. Areas that previously were flooded every fifty years can now expect that by 2080 they will be flooded for nine out of every ten years. Storms and heavy seas will batter coastal areas during the winter. The summers in Ireland and Britain will be longer and drier. Each decade there will be an average increase in temperature of more than .25 degrees Celsius. The top summer temperature in the south of England could reach 40 degrees Celsius. While some might see this as a blessing, their view is short-sighted. Such a major climate change would have a huge impact on agriculture and on the Irish landscape.[6] In November 2002 there was widespread flooding in Dublin, Meath and Cork. Floods used to occur approximately once every thirty years. They now come more often. They returned in 2004. While most scientists predict that as a result of global warming Irish summers will be warmer, other analysts predict that the future for Ireland may be the opposite.[7] They base their predictions on the fact that the melting of the Artic ice cap may interfere with, or even suspend, the Gulf Stream which keeps these islands warm. If this happens the effect would be to leave Ireland, and much of Northern Europe, substantially colder than at present.

Climate Change and the Spread of Diseases

According to the British Meteorological Office in 1998 the warmer climate has helped insects, mosquitoes and rodents expand their range and their ability to cause sickness to humans. Malaria, which is carried by the Anopheles mosquito, has now been found in southern Europe and also in Korea. Similarly, until a few decades ago, dengue fever was confined mainly to south-east Asia and the Caribbean. Now it is infecting people in Africa, Central and Latin America and the Indian subcontinent. The sad reality is that the poor once again will suffer most from the illnesses that follow in the wake of global warming.

In January 2004, Sir David King chided President George Bush for not taking seriously the threat to global security from global warming. In King's view, US climate policy is a bigger threat to the world than terrorism since 'as a consequence of continued warming, millions more people around the world may in future be exposed to the risk of hunger, drought, flooding and debilitating diseases such as malaria'.[8] During the same week an international team of scientists under the leadership of Dr Chris Thomas, Professor of Conservation Biology at Leeds University, claimed that global warming would cause the extinction of one million species by 2050.[9] While many people around the world are angry at the unwillingness of President Bush to address the issue of global warming, the record of Irish politicians in addressing this issue is equally irresponsible.

Kyoto and Ireland

At the UN-sponsored conference on climate change in Kyoto in 1997 scores of scientists from the International Panel on Climate Change (IPCC) called for a 60% reduction in the use of fossil fuel to reduce carbon emissions – our greenhouse emissions. Unfortunately the politicians, representing 160 countries, attending the meeting could only agree to a miserly 5.2% reduction below the 1990 levels to be achieved by 2010. From the scientific view this is minimal but at least it is a start. Unfortunately, within three months of coming into power, President George Bush decided that he would not ask the Senate of the United States to sign up to the protocol.

And what of Ireland? At Kyoto, Ireland was one of the few wealthy nations that actually received permission to increase its greenhouse gas emissions. We claimed that since we had not been industrialised in the nineteenth century we should be allowed more leeway than the other first-world counties. Thus, we were allowed to increase our greenhouse gas emissions by 13% above the 1990 levels by the year 2001. The leaps and bounds of the 'Celtic Tiger' during the mid-1990s meant that by 1998 we had already exceeded these greenhouse gas emission levels. In August 2000 the Environmental Protection Agency (EPA) published its report, 'Emissions of Atmospheric Pollutants in Ireland 1990–1998'. This stated that we had already exceeded our 2010 target by 1998; our greenhouse gas emissions had grown by 18% in eight years and the annual rate of increase in 1998 stood at 4%.

In response, the Department of the Environment published the 'National Climate Change Strategy' in order to curb greenhouse gas emissions. Among the initiatives mentioned were an unspecified tax on fossil fuel, the closure or conversion of the Moneypoint coal-fired generating power station and reductions in the number of animals in the national herd. The strategy document notes that 'transport is generally proving to be the most difficult sector in which to achieve controls on greenhouse gas emissions in most countries due to the rising vehicle numbers and increasing travel'.[10] Chapter 5 of the strategy document deals with transport in a vague and aspirational manner. The development of rail transport is mentioned on a few occasions but, for the authors of the strategy document, it is clear that 'transport' means 'road transport'. Ireland published its national strategy on climate change at the same time it decided to spend €20 billion on motorways! At the time of the publication of the strategy, I attempted to find out whether any government department or agency had calculated what increased greenhouse emissions would result from the new road-building programme. A helpful person at the National Roads Authority (name with author) informed me that the NRA had not quantified the increased greenhouse gas emissions since their Environmental Impact Studies (EIS) only examine the effect of motorway construction and predicted use on local levels of air pollution.

In July 2002 the Irish government produced another document in preparation for the World Summit on Sustainable Development, held in Johannesburg (August 26–September 4 2002). This second document, 'Making Ireland Sustainable', acknowledges that, according to the EPA, Ireland's emissions of greenhouse gases in 2000 was already 23.7% above the base-line 1990 levels and, given a 'business-as-usual' scenario, they would increase by 37% by 2010. The document is again 'heavy' on spin and aspiration. It informs its readers that 'it has always been recognised that, with no action, Ireland would rapidly and substantially exceed its [Kyoto] Protocol targets'.[11] It, therefore, goes on to state that 'significant action' is required over the decade to limit the rise in emissions to 13%.[12]

Towards the end of 2002 the Irish government became increasingly aware that the failure to take effective steps to curb greenhouse gas emissions (either by way of a tax on fossil fuel or a subsidy to promote alternative energy sources) could result in financial penalties. Research by the EPA and consultants DIW Berlin indicated that by 2001 Ireland had increased emissions by 30% over the 1990 base-line and that, if present policies continue, the increase will be 60% by 2012. The mindset of Government departments is clearly to put the needs of industry ahead of everything else.[13] Since fines are part of the Kyoto Protocol, Ireland could be facing penalties as high as €4.8 billion. An alternative would be to purchase permits from other counties whose emissions levels are below those approved under Kyoto. It is estimated that this would cost €200 million per year.[14]

Depletion of the Ozone Layer

Chemicals produced by industrial activity, especially CFCs, are interfering with the way ozone is created and broken down, threatening to reduce its concentration in the upper atmosphere. The ozone layer filters out much of the sun's ultraviolet radiation. In recent years a 'hole' the size of the United States has appeared each spring over Antarctica. For the past two years a similar, though not as extensive, depletion has also been detected over the Arctic. Because of the depletion of the ozone layer human populations are being exposed to higher levels of potentially dangerous forms of radiation that may lead to skin cancer and eye disease. It will also lead to smaller crops and lower timber yields.

Land

Poor land management, overgrazing, chemical agriculture, deforestation and population pressures have caused soil erosion and desertification on an unprecedented scale. About 3,500 million hectares – an area the size of North and South America combined – are affected by desertification. Each year at least another six million hectares of land are irretrievably lost to desertification and a further 21 million hectares are so degraded that crop production is severely affected. World wide about 35 billion tons of soil are lost each year. Unfortunately, most of this damage is in the two-third world. In the Philippines, for example, the bishops, in a pastoral letter entitled 'What is happening to our beautiful land?', estimate that 100,000 hectares one metre thick is being lost each year, mainly as a result of deforestation, mono-cropping and planting in hilly areas which are unsuitable for annual crops.

In recent decades most of the investment in agriculture, especially by multilateral lending agencies like the World Bank, was used for mega-projects like irrigation or for farm machinery, agricultural credit or petrochemicals. The form of agriculture that has been promoted is extremely expensive because it is dependant on foreign loans and imported petrochemicals and seeds. It benefits the oil companies, manufacturers of farm equipment, banks and large farmers. But it has further impoverished the poor and, in many parts of the world, it has destroyed the fertility of the soil. On-going research has demonstrated that in these regions of the world the most successful programmes are those aimed at halting desertification and soil erosion. These are successful if they are local, small in scale and run by those who are intimately affected. They are also relatively low-cost initiatives. They involve tree planting, improved farming techniques and, most critically, small scale organic farming and better land use. Unfortunately, very little funding has been made available by governments or multilateral lending agencies for such programmes, whereas millions of dollars have been poured into research institutes such as the International Rice Research Institute in Los Banos near Manila in the Philippines, which has pioneered and promoted chemical agriculture.

Water

Consider another issue – water. Everyone needs water, whether rich or poor, and we need the equivalent of three litres of water a day. Yet human activity is polluting water in the oceans, rivers, aquifers and lakes. More than 97% of the water on earth is seawater. Of the remaining 3%, only 1% is available for human use in agriculture, industry or for domestic purposes. Every day 6,000 children die from waterborne diseases, far more than were killed in one day on 9/11 in New York and Washington. And human access to this water is very inequitable. In preparation for its 2002 conference in Johannesburg, the United Nations Environmental Programme published a 'Global Environment Outlook' which estimated that over 1,200 million people do not have access to an adequate supply of potable water and some 2,500 million people are without proper sanitation. The most chilling aspect of the report is the prediction that, unless effective measures are taken, by 2032 two out of three people on the planet will be suffering from water stress.

The above report also predicted that most wars in the twenty-first century will be fought not over oil but over water. In the Middle East there are numerous potential flash points along the Tigris and Euphrates, especially between Turkey, Iran and Iraq. The same is true between India and Pakistan and between India and Bangladesh, and also in Africa. I have written more extensively about these potential conflicts in *Dying for Water* (2003). Not only between countries but also within countries there will be a scramble for water. In June 2005 Qui Baoxing, a minister in the Chinese government, indicated that 100 of China's 660 cities are facing an extreme water shortage. In northern China the Yellow River has been so exploited that for most of the year it fails to reach the ocean. Even the Yangtze, which supplies water for one-twelfth of the world's population, is under pressure from dams and from water pollution from the huge cities along its banks which do not properly treat their municipal waste. Because the Chinese government is slow to address pollution by tightening factory emissions and reducing logging at the head waters, the situation is likely to deteriorate even further.[15] The Ganges, the Elbe and the Mersey are all also heavily polluted.[16]

In *Dying for Water* I also examine the destruction of the oceans through over-fishing and the destruction of ecosystems like coral reefs and mangrove forests. There are also major concerns about the contamination of the oceans close to the continental landmasses with human, agricultural and radioactive waste (much of which is toxic and carcinogenic). Many of the seas are polluted almost beyond repair. The Irish Sea is the most radioactive body of water in the world. The North Sea and the Mediterranean are polluted and the Aral Sea has been totally destroyed. Pollution of the oceans and rivers affects us all. The hydrological cycle recycles this water back onto our lands and food supply and ultimately into our very cells.

Species Extinction

Tropical forests once covered 20% of the land area of the earth. This is no longer so; they are disappearing at an extraordinary rate. An area greater in size than the United Kingdom is cleared and destroyed each year through logging, cattle ranching and the opening up of lands for agriculture, itself due to the fact that much of the arable land in tropical countries is in the hands of a small percentage of the elite. Such destruction of the tropical forests will have many ill effects on agriculture and human livelihood. It will affect the health and productivity of nearby rivers and estuaries and local and global climatic patterns. Perhaps the greatest tragedy of all is the mega-extinction of species that is following in the wake of the destruction of the forests. Already tens of thousands of species have been lost. E.O. Wilson, a Harvard biologist, estimates that we are losing 27,000 species each year. Many experts would consider this to be a conservative estimate. Wilson warns that this destruction of species will soar as the last remaining areas of the tropical forests are exploited and destroyed. He considers that 'ruling out nuclear war, the worst thing now taking place is the loss of genetic diversity'.[17]

So, we are not only destroying ourselves, we are destroying animal life, and not just individual animals but whole species of animals. They are our cousins on this planet. If we don't make this a home for ourselves and for them then, in a sense, we can't talk in any way about hospitality. Here in Ireland the ones we are losing are mainly the bird species. Most of my generation grew up listening to the sound of the lark. I have often talked to students in schools around Ireland about the lark and we play the lovely music – 'The Lark in the Clear Air' or 'A Lark Ascending'. But how many people in Ireland today have ever heard a lark? Probably only those living in the west of Ireland.

If the present rate of extinction continues, fifty per cent or even more of all the life forms on earth could be extinguished during the next few decades. Norman Myers, a British biologist and author of an important work on the rainforest, *The Ultimate Resource* (1996), considers that the present 'extinction spasm' is the greatest setback to life's abundance and diversity since the first flickering of life emerged almost four billion years ago. Extinction on such a scale is so horrendous that it is difficult to grasp. Our inability to comprehend the magnitude of what is happening is increased by the fact that few of the people who make the economic and political decisions that have such world-wide repercussions have any intimate knowledge of the rainforest or any other ecosystem on planet earth. It is of course a fact that generally this mega-extinction is not directly willed as such. Humans have in fact only consciously set about extinguishing one species, smallpox. The mega-extinction is a direct result of the expansion of the industrial economy into fragile ecosystems such as rainforests.

Summary of the Ecological Devastation of our Planet
One could continue to pile depressing data on depressing data but what I have presented above provides a sufficient framework with which to begin to appreciate what is happening to our planet and what is happening locally in Ireland. Human industrial activity is changing the chemistry of the air and the water, altering the hydrological cycles and upsetting the entire self-renewing pattern of nature that has taken billions of years to emerge. Only now are we beginning to wake up to the consequences of our activity. There is, of course, a deep irony in what has happened. Western human beings set out, through the mastery of science and, its handmaid, technology to make human

beings as independent of nature as possible and to ensure that nature was subservient to human decisions. While this project has provided greater comforts for a small segment of humanity it has impoverished the vast majority of people in the two-thirds world and is now threatening the very survival of many of the earth's creatures, including human beings.

Towards a Global Ethic

How do we respond to this extraordinary destruction of life? You would think that the pro-life Churches would mourn this devastation of God's creation. Yet largely all we hear is silence. Ingrained in our imagination is: 'You can always put off these things – the poor will always be with you.' But the planet, its beauty and fruitfulness will not always be with us. Because the reality of extinction and the processes by which it is taking place is removed from our daily awareness, our usual moral and ethical categories fail to even register what is happening or to respond in a concerned way. Our moral principles can deal with suicide, homicide and even genocide but we have no way of dealing with biocide. Thomas Berry has attempted to broaden the parameters of our moral universe and to enable us to comprehend what is taking place in our times and, by developing wider moral categories, enable us to respond. Berry insists that:

> Extinction is an ethical concept. It is not at all like the killing of individual life forms that can be renewed by the normal process of reproduction ... nor is it something that can be remedied ... nor is it something which affects only our own generation. No! It is an absolute and final act for which there is no remedy on earth or in heaven.[18]

The labour, care and energy expended over billions of years to bring forth such a gorgeous earth is being negated in less than a century in the search for what we consider to be progress towards a 'better' life in a 'better' world! There is a particular urgency about halting species extinction. As I wrote in *The Death of Life: The Horror of Extinction* (2004):

If this generation does not act no future generation will be able to undo the damage that this generation has caused to the planet. It is an extraordinary and awesome moment that the behaviour of a single generation of humans can have such a profound and irreversible impact, not just on human history, but on the life of the planet as well. Lastly, species extinction cannot continue with impunity. Sooner or later extinction will rob our planet of the ability to sustain many forms of life, possibly even our own.[19]

Ecological Conversion and its Virtues

Pope John Paul II had insightful things to say about our responsibility towards the environment which have been totally overlooked. On 1 January 1990 he issued 'Peace with God the Creator, Peace with all Creation' in which he stated that 'Christians, in particular, know that their responsibility within creation and their duty towards God the Creator are an essential part of their faith' (par. 14). He noted in the same document that 'modern society will find no solution to the ecological problems unless it takes a serious look at its lifestyle' (par. 13). He continued that 'simplicity, moderation and discipline, as well as a spirit of sacrifice, must become part of everyday life, lest all suffer the negative consequence of the careless habits of a few' (par. 13). Eleven years later in 2001, Pope John Paul II's environmental critique was much more forthright and ominous; he used extraordinary language to state:

In our time humans have devastated wooded plains and valleys, polluted the waters, deformed the earth's habitat, made their air unbreathable, upset the hydrological and atmospheric systems, blighted green spaces, implemented uncontrolled forms of industrialisation, humiliating – to use the words of Dante Alighieri – the earth, the flowerbed that is our dwelling. … It is necessary, therefore, to stimulate and sustain the 'ecological conversion' which over these last decades have made humanity more sensitive when faced with the catastrophe towards which it is moving.[20]

Unfortunately this call to conversion has, for the most part, fallen on deaf ears because people in vital positions in politics, economics, the media and religion fail to assess the ecological impact of their activities. One might be tempted to dismiss the late Pope's words as having more to do with apocalyptic religious language than with science. But his words are substantiated by the Millennium Ecosystems Report published shortly before the Pope died. The authors of the report issued the stark warning that human activity is putting such a strain on the natural functions of the earth that the ability of the planet's ecosystems to sustain future generations (of humans) can no longer be taken for granted. This report cannot be easily brushed aside. It was collated under the direction of Robert Watson, the chief scientist at the World Bank, aided by over 1,300 scientists from almost 100 countries.

What are some of the elements that might form this 'ecological' conversion called for by the late Pope? Contemporary social theology reminds us that we need to develop right relationships in the social and ecological sphere to ensure that all members of the earth community enjoy the habitat and resources that they need to flourish. Our teaching on sustainability reminds us that the earth is finite and that we must live in a way that is fair and just to future generations of humans and other creatures.

Bio-responsibility

Let me first highlight bio-responsibility. This extends the covenant of justice and hospitality to include all other life forms as beloved creatures of God and as expressions of God's presence, wisdom, power and glory in our world. We are very focused on the human. In a recent compendium of Catholic social teaching containing over three hundred pages, the section on ecology was only eighteen pages. This is a total inversion. We are guests of the planet. It is the planet that created life forms and that gives off the oxygen that allows us to breathe. It is the planet that created our cell structure that allowed our ancestors to come out of the ocean and wander around on the earth. If we pollute or destroy the water, the air and the earth then there isn't any great future for us or for other species.

Humility

A second virtue is humility. As humans we need to stand with humility on this planet as an antidote to technological arrogance. Many people would want us to believe that we can manage the world with some new technologies. The truth is that we know very little about our world. For example, we don't know how many species live on the planet with us. There might be five million, there might be ten million, there might even be a hundred million. We simply do not know; yet in our conceit we think we can master creation.

Generosity

At the heart of hospitality is generosity, actions that share the fruitfulness of our planet and the earth's riches with all humanity, future generations and all God's creatures. We must promote the common good of all. A core principle of Catholic social teaching is that the goods of the world are meant for all the peoples of the world. I would simply add 'and all the creatures of the world' too.

Frugality

Fourthly, we need frugality. I have already drawn attention to the fact that our planet can afford the affluence of one-fifth of its population; it cannot support the affluence of 6.6 billion. Frugality invites us to restrain our economic production and consumption patterns, especially in rich countries, for the sake of the welfare of all creatures and the earth. Jesus warned us that we will never achieve happiness by accumulating material things. The virtual world that our economies have created has dislocated us from everything – the texture of the earth itself, but also the texture of community life that makes life liveable and enjoyable and pleasant.

Solidarity

Then of course we need the virtue of solidarity. This virtue was much beloved of the late John Paul II. In his encyclical letter *Sollicitudo rei Socialis* (1987) he describes solidarity as 'not a vague compassion or shallow distress at the misfortunes of many people, both far and near. On the contrary, it is a firm and persevering determination to commit oneself to the common good; that is to say, the good of all and of each individual, because we are all really responsible for all' (art. 43). In the context of the ecological crisis, solidarity acknowledges that we are bound together as members of the earth community. We are responsible for the well being of the poor and of all creation. Since in our origins we are linked together, our destinies too are also intimately linked. Either we will pass on a fruitful, beautiful and vibrant planet to nurture the well being of all future generations and creatures, or we will be forced to live amid the ruins of both our technological and natural world. Thus, solidarity cannot just be with our fellow humans; it has to be with all our fellow creatures.

We need a different paradigm from which to understand solidarity. We talk about us 'caring for the earth' when, in fact, it is the earth that cares for us. We regard the world as good and yet in our Christian tradition, both Catholic and reformed, we have an ambivalent position towards solidarity with the earth. I am old enough to have said Mass in the pre-Vatican II era. On the fourth Sunday before Christmas we prayed, 'teach us to despise the things of earth and to love the things of heaven'. Why should we worry about CFCs, toxic waste and destruction of the environment if we are to despise the things of the earth. Even in one of the loveliest and, to me, one of the most important prayers, the Rosary, we refer to 'mourning and weeping in this valley of tears'. This is not a valley of tears; there is a tear dimension to life but the world is an allurement to us. We need to be enchanted by it and there is every reason we should be and can be; our music and our poetry should enchant us. Another image that we have to divest ourselves of is that we are 'stewards of the earth'. Who are we stewards for? Are we stewards for God? But God is part of the earth. We are hardly stewards for other creatures if we don't know how many of them there are, and we are not behaving as stewards for future generations. Instead we must really see that this is an enchanting world.

Thanksgiving

Central to hospitality towards the earth is the virtue of thanksgiving or gratitude. We are a people who are to give thanks to God for the wonders of God's love in Christ and the blessings of all creation. At the heart of our liturgy is Eucharist – 'giving thanks'. We give thanks through the mediation of bread and wine, the fruits of the earth and the work and toil of men and women. We could reconnect hugely with the earth if every time we broke bread in the Eucharist we talked about sharing that bread. But also we should ask, 'where is this bread coming from?' In 1984 the International Commission for English in the Liturgy (ICEL) published a Eucharistic Prayer, the Preface of which centred on creation:

> Blessed are you, strong and faithful God.
> All your works, the height and depth,
> echo the silent music of your praise.
> In the beginning your Word summoned light;
> night withdrew and creation dawned.
> As ages passed unseen,
> waters gathered on the face of the Earth
> and life appeared.
> When the times had at last grown full
> and the earth had ripened in abundance,
> you created in your image humankind,
> the crown of all creation.

In our liturgies we must proclaim the story of the universe and the story of creation. Where do we as humans fit into creation? Extend your hand. It represents the period of life on the planet. Now take a nail file and rub just a slight bit from the top of your index finger. That's humankind's presence – a mere 2.4 million years. Until we begin to see ourselves as part of that community of creation in all its longitude and in its present structure we won't have gratitude to all creation. We must always remember that we depend on creation. In our Catholic tradition, Francis has been declared patron of ecology because he regarded all of creation as brothers and sisters. There is also the Benedictine tradition of care, respect and stability.

Thus, we must go beyond the limited notion of stewardship to a wonder-filled celebration of fellowship and a recognition that all is gift. This is captured by the American author, Wendell Berry, in his book *The Gift of Good Land*. Land is not just about money, or monetary value; land is about community. Berry puts it like this:

> To live we must daily break the body and shed the blood of creation. When we do this knowingly, lovingly, skilfully and reverently it is a sacrament. When we do it ignorantly, greedily and destructively, it is a desecration. It is such a desecration we condemn ourselves to spiritual and moral loneliness and others to want.[21]

Conclusion

Conversion to eco-hospitality is awakened by contemplation and prayer. Such prayer acknowledges our awareness of the gifts that we have received. The focus on such prayer is not just the concern of New Age communities. St Basil, one of the key figures of the Patristic Era, had such a sensibility. It is with his prayer that this chapter concludes:

> O God, enlarge within us a sense of fellowship with all living beings, our brothers and sisters the animals, to whom thou gavest the earth as their home in common with us.

We remember with shame that in the past we have exercised the high dominion of man (and woman) with ruthless cruelty, so that the voice of the earth, which should have gone up to thee in song, has been a groan of travail. May we realise that they live not for us alone, but for themselves and for thee and that they too love the sweetness of life.

Bibliography

Berry, W., *The Gift of Good Land*, San Francisco: North Point Press, 1981.

George, S., *The Debt Boomerang*, London: Pluto, 1992.

McDonagh, S., *The Death of Life: The Horror of Extinction*, Dublin: Columba Press, 2004.

    Patenting Life? Stop: Is Corporate Greed Forcing us to Eat Genetically Engineered Food?, Dublin: Dominican Publications, 2003.

    Dying for Water, Dublin: Veritas, 2003.

    Why are we Deaf to the Cry of the Earth?, Dublin: Veritas, 2001.

    Greening the Christian Millennium, Dublin: Dominican Publications, 1999.

    Passion for the Earth, London: Geoffrey Chapman, 1994.

    The Greening of the Church, London: Geoffrey Chapman, 1990.

    To Care for the Earth, London: Geoffrey Chapman, 1986.

Wilson, E.O., *Biophilia*, Harvard: Harvard University Press, 1984.

Notes

1. S. McDonagh, *Passion for the Earth*, London: Geoffrey Chapman, pp. 2–3.
2. United Nations Childrens' Fund (UNICEF), *The State of the World's Children*, Oxford University Press, 1989.
3. John Vidal, 'Global Warming is Greater than Predicted' (Study), *The Irish Times*, 27 October 2000.
4. Paul Brown, 'Global Warming Melts Glaciers and Produces many Unstable Lakes', *The Guardian*, 17 April 2002.
5. Sir David King, 'Clean Air Act', *The Guardian Supplement*, 24 November 2005, p. 15.
6. Ann Cahill, 'Days of Drought and Deluge Loom', *The Irish Examiner*, 1 May 2002, p. 5.
7. William Calvin, *A Brain for All Seasons: Evolution and Abrupt Climate Change*, Chicago: University of Chicago Press, 2002.
8. Steve Connor, 'US Climate Policy is a Bigger Threat to the World than Terrorism', *The Independent*, 9 January 2004, p. 1.
9. Paul Brown, 'An Unnatural Disaster', *The Guardian*, 8 January 2004, p. 1.
10. Department of the Environment, *National Climate Change Strategy*, Dublin: Government Publications, 2000, p. 24.

11. Environmental Protection Agency, *Making Ireland Sustainable,* Wexford: Johnstown Castle, 2002.
12. 'Meeting Kyoto Commitment seen as a "Core Challenge"', *The Irish Times,* 26 July 2002, p. 5.
13. Liam Reid, 'Kyoto May Cost State 5 Billion Euro', *The Sunday Tribune,* 2 February 2002, p. 1.
14. Liam Reid, 'Kyoto Shortfall to Cost Government 185 Million Euro', *The Irish Times,* 31 December 2004, p. 4.
15. Jonathan Watts, '"100 Chinese Cities Face Water Crisis", says Minister,' *The Guardian,* 8 June 2005.
16. *The Sunday Times Magazine,* 1 July 1990.
17. E.O. Wilson, *Biophilia,* Harvard: Harvard University Press, 1984, p. 122.
18. Thomas Berry, *Riverdale Papers,* Vol 8, New York: Riverdale, Riverdale Centre for Religious Studies (Unpublished).
19. Sean McDonagh, *The Death of Life: The Horror of Extinction,* Dublin: The Columba Press, 2002, p. 157.
20. John Paul II, 'God made Man the Steward of Creation', General Audience, 17 January 2001, par. 3.
21. Wendall Berry, *The Gift of Good Land,* San Francisco: North Point Press, 1981, p. 281.

Recovering Hospitality as a Christian Tradition

Christine D. Pohl

Introduction

Offering welcome to strangers is at the heart of the Gospel and Christian identity. In contemporary life, however, it is largely overlooked as a significant Christian practice. By examining the rich resources of the biblical texts and the historical Christian tradition, the life-giving dimensions of hospitality can be explored and its relevance for current concerns demonstrated.

There are three distinct but interrelated strands of tradition that inform our present thinking about recovering hospitality as a vibrant practice. Firstly, the biblical tradition and the tradition of the Church offer wonderful resources. Secondly, Irish culture, especially the Celtic tradition, has given a special place to and has developed a rich spirituality around hospitality. And thirdly, the St John of God communities recognise hospitality as their central gift, practice or charism.

The focus of my research and writing has been on the biblical tradition of welcoming strangers and on how understandings of hospitality were expressed in several streams of Church tradition.[1] Although I have much to learn about the Celtic tradition, I did discover the importance of Irish monasticism for the recovery of the moral significance of hospitality in the United States. Peter Maurin, co-founder of the Catholic Worker Movement in the 1930s, was deeply influenced by Irish monasticism and I am persuaded that it was the Catholic Worker Movement, more than any other community, which has helped Americans see that hospitality to vulnerable strangers is central to Christian identity. Only in the last year have I been introduced to the riches of the St John of God tradition. I deeply regret that I did not know about it earlier in my work on hospitality. In their history and current practice, St John of God communities demonstrate the life-giving character of a commitment to welcoming the most vulnerable people.

The New Testament theologian Krister Stendahl once commented that 'wherever, whenever, however the kingdom manifests itself, it is welcome'.[2] Hospitality is, or should be, at the centre of Christian life and discipleship because hospitality is at the centre of the Gospel. When we read the Scriptures attentive to themes and expressions of hospitality, we discover that they are everywhere. People often overlook the moral and theological significance of hospitality, but a life of hospitality is basic to what it means to be Jesus' disciples. In what follows, we will consider some of the resources in the biblical tradition and in Church history related to hospitality. We will reflect briefly on what happened to the practice in Church life, and then explore what the tradition can teach us and why it is so important today for us to recover the practice of welcoming strangers.

The Biblical Tradition of Hospitality

There is a rich tradition of hospitality in the Scriptures – it is surprising how many images of God, stories and teachings in the Bible are related to hospitality. The story begins in a garden in which God is a gracious host who makes a wonderful place for humankind. In Exodus, God provides for a previously enslaved people as they wander through the wilderness, and feeds them with manna everyday. At the end of the story, in Revelation, Jesus stands at the door knocking and promises to everyone who opens the door to him that he will come in and join them for a meal.

Few images in the Gospels recur with more frequency than those of Jesus as host, guest or stranger. He is a generous host who makes room for people, a needy and sometimes unwelcome stranger, and an unpredictable guest (e.g. Matt 14:13-21, 15:32-39, 19:13-15; Lk 7:36-50, 9:51-56, 14:1-14, 19:1-10, 24:13-35; Jn 1:1-18, 4:1-42, 6:1-14, 12:1-8, 13:1-20, 21:1-14). Amazingly, Jesus even describes himself as bread, the bread of life, the bread that has come down from heaven. So not only host and guest, Jesus is also our nourishment, our strength and our sustenance (Jn 6:25-59). And in this light, we can consider the extraordinary enactment of hospitality in the Eucharist, where we remember the costly welcome we have received into the kingdom, and where we are regularly welcomed to the table of the kingdom. Hospitality condenses much of the meaning of the Gospel.

Hospitality in the Scriptures and in the Christian tradition is closely associated with God's deep concern for people without power and resources. The wonderful passage in Deuteronomy 10 combines a description of God's character and work with expectations for the behaviour of God's people:

> For the Lord your God is God of gods and Lord of lords, the great God, mighty and awesome, who is not partial and takes no bribe, who executes justice for the orphan and the widow, and who loves the strangers, providing them food and clothing. You shall also love the stranger, for you were strangers in the land of Egypt (Deut 10:17-19).[3]

In chapter 24 of Deuteronomy,[4] the implications of God's love for the vulnerable is more fully spelled out – God's own people must make sure that resident aliens, fatherless children and widows are protected from injustice, and that they have access to food and to the things necessary for life. The identity and well being of the people of God are wrapped up in how they care for those on the margins – those without voice, power or resources.

It is not difficult to make the connection between vulnerable populations of biblical times and the populations with whom many of us work today – people with serious disabilities, fatherless families, frail elderly people, abused and neglected children, those with grave illnesses, migrant workers, ethnic minorities, refugees, or the long-term unemployed. In the New Testament, we can see how Jesus reached out to many of these same people and made a place for them in his new community. He asked that his faithful followers be attentive and open, appreciative of the folks that most people don't have time for, folks that are ordinarily overlooked in the rosters of the important and impressive. What is perhaps most startling of all in Jesus' teaching about the people on the margins – the sick, the imprisoned, the hungry and the strangers – is that ministry to the least of them is somehow ministry to him.

Jesus' understanding of hospitality was very unconventional. He was a willing guest at dinner parties hosted by the wrong kind of people, and he graciously welcomed children, people with mental illness, the ritually unclean, and those caught in patterns of sin and self-destruction (e.g. Lk 5:27-32, 7:36-50, 18:15-17, 19:1-10; Jn 4:1-42). He challenged the well placed in his society to rethink their own guest lists and to have parties for those who didn't seem to have much to offer, and then to let God do the blessing. In ancient times, people believed that hospitality was one of the pillars of morality on which the universe rested. Before inns, hotels and restaurants, everyone away from home needed hospitality, whether or not they had resources. Thus, for most societies hospitality was highly valued as a form of mutual aid. It was an important practice oriented toward care for strangers. It meant welcoming the stranger into one's personal space – generously offering food and shelter, protection and respect.

For the early Christians, hospitality was important for a number of additional reasons. Their practice of hospitality looked different from the surrounding society, because of the One who had welcomed them. Early followers of Jesus took seriously the Old Testament concerns about protection of and care for the sojourner or resident alien – along with the poor and vulnerable. They remembered the wonderful story in Genesis 18 when Abraham and Sarah welcomed three strangers and, in the context of hospitality, discovered that the strangers were angels who had come with a promise and with blessing. Many centuries after Abraham and Sarah, in the letter to the Hebrews, those early Christians were reminded: 'Do not neglect to show hospitality to strangers, for by doing that some have entertained angels without knowing it' (Heb 13:2). The followers of Jesus encouraged one another to practice hospitality ungrudgingly (1 Pet 4:9) – an early recognition that it must have been difficult to live a life of welcome and not sometimes resent the trouble, the challenges, or the sacrifice involved.

In particular, the early Christians offered hospitality because they had themselves been welcomed. Paul writes in Romans 15:7: 'Welcome one another ... just as Christ has welcomed you.' To us this sounds nice, but not revolutionary. But when we recognise that those early congregations were composed of an unsettling mixture of rich and poor, and of Gentiles and Jews, we quickly realise that it could not have been easy to welcome fellow believers, much less strangers and outsiders. They would have remembered clearly just how costly Jesus' welcome to them had been. And so we begin to understand that this was indeed a very revolutionary request from Paul: 'Welcome one another ... just as Christ has welcomed you' – at the cost of his own life. Jesus' teaching, especially in Matthew 25:31-46, makes care for vulnerable people a very personal issue. In this passage, central to the hospitality tradition, he explains, 'just as you did it to one of the least of these' brothers and sisters of mine – inasmuch as you have fed the hungry person, welcomed the stranger, visited the sick and imprisoned – 'you did it to me'. And inasmuch as you have neglected any of these, you have done it to me. The ancient Church took his words seriously and Christian believers opened their doors because in some mysterious way, it might be Jesus who was knocking; they respected the poor person, because that man or woman might just be Jesus in 'distressing disguise'.[5] In addition, there is a very disconcerting passage in Luke 14 about who one's preferred guests should be. At what must have been a very awkward dinner party, Jesus turned to his host and said:

> When you give a luncheon or a dinner, do not invite your friends or your brothers or your relatives or rich neighbours, in case they may invite you in return, and you would be repaid. But when you give a banquet, invite the poor, the crippled, the lame and the blind. And you will be blessed, because they cannot repay you, for you will be repaid at the resurrection of the righteous (Lk 14:12-14).

Jesus challenges those who would follow him to rethink to whom they pay attention and to reconsider what kinds of people they want at their events or seated at their dinner tables. It is not those the world values, but rather the ones the world overlooks, and assumes have little to offer, that must be invited. While Jesus and the early Church continued to value welcome to family and friends, they pushed the circle of care outward and pressed the community of love to grow bigger.

The early Christians struggled with welcome. If in Christ, 'there is no longer Jew or Greek, there is no longer slave or free, there is no longer male and female' (Gal 3:28), what implications would that have for their communal life? If rich and poor were welcome at the same table, how would that extraordinary welcome be translated into how they treated one another? One of the practices that distinguished the early Church was how these first Christians crossed the boundaries of status and class that so defined their larger society. Jews and Greeks, and rich and poor created a new life together. Because meals were highly socially bounded – in other words, people only ate with people like themselves – shared meals in the Church community became an important site for working through these issues. This is evident in the book of Acts and in several of the epistles. The larger society found such hospitable Christian behaviour and relationships both challenging and disturbing.

Hospitality was important to the early Church for several other reasons. In the first generations, before the New Testament was written down, the Gospel was spread by believers who travelled from place to place sharing the Good News. They depended on the hospitality of Christians or 'seekers of the truth' in these places, and the welcome offered to them and to the Gospel message was fully intertwined. Hospitality was also important in those early years because of persecution; when believers had to flee, they were dependent on other Christians to welcome them into their households. Additionally, in the first generations, believers gathered in homes for worship and for regular shared meals. In this context, rich and poor broke bread together, Jews and Gentiles shared in one another's homes and lives. The resultant transformation was deeply personal and the community was vibrant. Physical needs were met in the context of community; new relationships were formed that gave people new families and support, and a new identity was forged.

These practices were so unusual and important to Christian identity that in the first centuries Christian apologists, or those who defended Christian faith to pagan rulers and leaders, used their way of life as proof of the truth of their message. In his first apology to the emperor (c. AD 155) Justin Martyr described the transformed lives of Christians to help pagan persecutors understand the power and truth of the Gospel:

> We who valued above all things the acquisition of wealth and possessions, now bring what we have into a common stock, and communicate [to share] with everyone in need; we who hated and destroyed one another, and on account of their different manners would not live with men of a different tribe [literally, 'would not use the same hearth or fire'] now, since the coming of Christ, live familiarly with them, and pray for our enemies.[6]

He explained that those who had previously despised one another and who would not sit down together at a meal now lived as family. In chapter 67 of his 'Apology', Justin described the Christian community's weekly practice of collecting offerings and depositing them with the leader who cares for 'the orphans and widows, and those who, through sickness or any other cause, are in want, and those who are in bonds, and the strangers sojourning among us, and in a word takes care of all who are in need'.[7]

While we should not romanticise this early period, it was a vibrant time in the life of the Church. Here we see Christians leading the way in inclusion, in crossing boundaries, in giving attention to the poor and broken – and not just in terms of handouts, but in terms of welcoming people into the centre of their lives and communities. As the Church grew and the persecutions lessened, and as the political rulers became more favourably inclined to Christianity, the Church's responsibility for the poor, the sick and for strangers actually increased. Its ministry came to be seen as public service, and by the latter part of the fourth century, the Church has significant social welfare responsibilities.

During this period we see the development of hospitals, clearly an attempt to make hospitality and care more available and predictable for the sick, for strangers and pilgrims and for the poor. This was a mixed blessing – an extraordinary array of hospitals were founded, but care for the poor and for strangers was increasingly offered at a distance from home and congregational life. People received care, but they were not necessarily incorporated into community. It took a long time for Christians to realise how problematic this shift would become.

The story of hospitality is a very complex one, but it is important to notice how closely identified Christians were with loving and respectful care for poor people and for strangers in these early centuries, and how hard they worked to cross status boundaries. It is also important to remember how implicated those early Christians were in creating institutions and structures that, while helpful in some ways, soon made it harder to live out some of their deepest commitments to respect and to shared life in community. But over these centuries, the Church struggled to hold together care and respect, and personal and communal responses to need.

In the fourth century, Church leaders articulated what was distinctive about Christian hospitality. Greek and Roman understandings of hospitality stressed reciprocal obligations between benefactor and recipient and emphasised the worthiness and goodness of recipients rather than their need. Hospitality was often calculated to benefit the benefactor, the host. The Church criticised such practice, calling such hospitality 'ambitious,' because it was offered for 'advantage'[8] and left out the very people who most needed welcome.

Church leaders argued that rather than entertaining persons who seemed to have something to offer, and thereby gaining earthly advantage from their hospitality, Christians were deliberately to welcome those who seemingly brought little to the encounter (echoes of Luke 14 and Matthew 25). Actually, there would be blessing and benefit, but it came from God. Accordingly for people like Jerome, John Chrysostom and Lactantius, hospitality meant extending to strangers a quality of kindness usually reserved for friends and family. Their focus was on strangers in need, the lowly and abject, those who, on first appearance, seemed to have little to offer. Lactantius finally equated hospitality with justice when he said: 'But in what does the nature of justice consist than in our affording to strangers through kindness, that which we render to our own relatives through affection'.[9]

The temptation, however, when welcoming those who did not seem to have much to offer, was to feel superior and to lose respect for them just because they were dependent. Leaders throughout the tradition had some sharp warnings for the Christians of their day and their words continue to speak to us. John Chrysostom wrote extensively on hospitality in the fourth and fifth centuries. He challenged his parishioners to welcome poor and vulnerable people personally, even as he and they worked to create hospitals and hospices, and to feed thousands of hungry people every day. He was convinced that within the practice of hospitality, Christians could meet the needs of poor people and strangers while still respecting their dignity as persons. He repeatedly warned his parishioners against holding a grudging spirit in the exercise of hospitality. Such an attitude is 'cruel and inhuman' because it is humiliating to the recipient.[10] He stressed the importance of respect and humility in offering help, criticising those who 'think themselves superior to the recipients, and often despise them for the attention given to them'.[11] Here, it seems, Chrysostom has his finger on a particularly difficult problem in ministry and social service, in that while offering help, we can disrespect those who receive it, simply because of their weakness and need. Chrysostom understood the terrible power of those with resources who could choose to humiliate even as they provided help. It is an old problem that manifests itself in new ways in every generation, every agency and just about every social programme.

The Decline of Hospitality

While it is not particularly helpful to paint the early Church as a golden age, its understanding of hospitality and its practices were quite extraordinary. In those early centuries, hospitality involved an outreach to the poor and vulnerable that was embedded in congregational life. It involved regular shared meals that both surfaced and challenged status boundaries. It was shaped by careful and respectful attention to the poor and to strangers. Over the centuries, however, a number of developments caused shifts in emphasis in the practice of hospitality.

Christians grew wary of allowing care to be dependent on personal inclination and tried to make it more predictable and dependable. Christian responsibilities increased and leaders were concerned about meeting the needs of vast numbers of people. They struggled with the temptation to separate care from respect. Gradually, even among Christians, hospitality came to be associated with entertaining and reinforcing power among the rich, and with giving handouts to the poor at the gates of wealthy churches or household institutions. There were periodic attempts to recover a more biblical practice, and we see this in different parts of the Christian tradition, for example, in the work of St John of God and in some of the Protestant reformers. But in the last several centuries, because the practice of hospitality had become so corrupted, the emphasis shifted to individual rights and a deliberate effort to establish more anonymity in donor/recipient relationships as a way of preserving the recipient's dignity. There was a simultaneous commitment to becoming much more methodical or systematic in meeting needs, and increased professionalisation and specialisation in care giving.

These developments had very mixed consequences, but one significant result was that the importance of vulnerable people being held by a particular community and rooted in relationships where they had opportunities to share gifts and be accountable – something Christian tradition had understood so well – was lost.

Recovering Hospitality

Obviously we cannot simply replicate practices from an earlier period, and we should not be nostalgic for past times that were as troubled as they were good. But today we are plagued by the breakdown of families, an uncertainty about cultural moorings, and we see intense yearnings for community and belonging in many places. These are challenges that earlier generations of Christians faced, and to which they responded with profound and life-changing hospitality. So we may well be able to recover sections of the tradition and may benefit from reflecting on how the tradition speaks to our contemporary situation. What is it that the tradition offers us? Often it is the case that we already have learned these insights but the tradition reinforces our best insights with its hard-earned and longstanding wisdom. Certain features of contemporary life make a recovery of hospitality both urgent and important.

A return to the wisdom of the tradition is helpful even for those already persuaded of the importance of hospitality. The tradition helps us tease out some of the issues, temptations and blessings from a different angle, one deeply rooted in Christian identity. It also helps us see that our struggles are mostly not new; over the centuries, faithful followers have faced similar difficulties and worked to find good solutions. The tradition challenges us, even those of us committed to welcome, because almost everyone and every community has certain people or kinds of people it excludes.

During 2004 I was teaching in New Zealand and talking with a tribal chief from one of the Pacific islands. At one point, during an intensive course in the ethics of hospitality, he said to me: 'I'm not sure why we are focusing on this; doesn't everyone offer hospitality? In our culture it is a way of life.' I was taken by his comment and by how natural it was for him to welcome strangers and friends even when it was quite costly. But I asked him, 'Are there any people or communities that you don't welcome or your tribe excludes that the Christian tradition might suggest you need to reconsider because they too should be offered hospitality?' He responded thoughtfully, 'Well, of course'. And I realised that all of us have blind spots and patterns of exclusion that are rarely explored or challenged.

A recovery of the tradition is important in a culture that is increasingly frenetic and urban, globalised yet disconnected, relationally challenged and media saturated. In settings where families are fractured and so much effort is oriented to measurable results and efficiency, hospitality is a strong countervailing voice about treasuring life and relationships in the context of very local responses.

The tradition, in its best moments, challenges us to offer service with the deepest respect and attentiveness. As Philip Hallie observed about certain forms of assistance: 'There is a way of helping that fills their hands and breaks their hearts.'[12] We know from experience what that looks like – where physical needs are met but spirits are broken, where in the interest of fiscal responsibility or efficiency we humiliate people by intruding excessively in their lives, or we ask for more openness from them than we would ever ask of people of more substantial means. Or we treat people carelessly, making assumptions that aren't necessarily true. Sometimes condescension slips in as we distance ourselves from problems and predicaments.

So much of helping is shaped by a concern that we not be taken advantage of, that those in need do not misuse our systems. Obviously concerns about stewardship and responsibility are important, but as John Calvin warned his readers in the sixteenth century: 'Let us beware that we seek not cover for our stinginess under the shadow of prudence.' Instead, our inquiries should not be 'too exacting,' he said, but rather done with a 'humane heart, inclined to pity and compassion'.[13]

The tradition challenges us to see people who come to us not as embodied needs but as persons with stories and gifts. In the context of specialisation, it is easy to reduce people to a set of particular and isolated needs, address one or two of them but miss the person. Specialisation obviously has benefits; for instance, it allows us to help in focused ways that come out of our strengths and our training. But if the person as a human being disappears, we have not done anything good.

The wisdom of the tradition strongly challenges us to work to connect vulnerable people with a community where they can be supported and can also share their gifts. Everyone needs a community, a place in which their gifts are valued. The tradition reminds us over and over again of the important combination of accountability and support. What characterises the most vulnerable people, whether refugees, homeless people or people with disabilities, is that regular networks of support have often failed. More than anything, they need to be reconnected to a community.

The wisdom of the tradition is, of course, also marred by blind spots, awful exclusions and struggles. Hospitality must be held together with a commitment to justice and with efforts that work for justice at a structural or systemic level. The commitment to hospitality helped to give rise to the notion of human rights, but that is a story for another time. If concerns about justice, equality, respect and mutuality are not kept to the forefront, hospitality can easily become a way to legitimate hierarchy and injustice; it can help keep some people as permanently powerless, needy guests and allow the host role to be used as a way to hold on to power. But the tradition also has the internal resources to powerfully critique these deformations. The tradition of hospitality recognises the fragility of the practice itself.

Insights from the tradition suggest that we should look closely at our organisations, agencies or services – or at the parts for which we have responsibility. We may not be able to totally change them but we can continually ask about what small acts, small shifts in orientation, would create space and interactions that are more life-giving.

Sometimes it can be helpful to do a hospitality inventory – asking how does this place communicate to people that they are valued or that it is a safe place for them to gather the fragments of their lives and begin again? How does our organisation or community communicate a genuine respect that simultaneously supports and challenges people toward growth and transformation? Attention to the language we use to describe or address the people with whom we work is important, as is looking at the signs posted around our buildings, or even at how furniture is arranged in a room. It is depressingly humorous to see how easy it is to overlook inhospitable messages. I was involved for a number of years with a church that was committed to welcoming strangers and to crossing racial boundaries. We went through a rough period with vandalism, however, and one day as I drove up the church driveway I found a sign that said 'NO TRESPASSING'. No trespassing in a church – what does that communicate to strangers?

The tradition also warns us to be careful not to hold on to the role of host too tightly, and to readily assume the role of guest at times. We need to help people see how important it is to allow others to be hosts and to honor the resources they have to share. This is a challenge for well-placed, well-educated and well-intentioned people, who often need to be reminded that resources should not and do not flow only in one direction.

In fact, the tradition warns us that the practice of hospitality is vulnerable to a number of temptations. Our acts of hospitality do not necessarily diminish our temptations to power, greed, self-aggrandisement or ambition. Hospitality can be a slippery avenue to these things – that is what corrupted it in the past and why it so often, even today, degenerates into entertaining. Entertaining puts the focus on the host; hospitality is focused on the guest. Because hospitality is effective and because it is such a profound aspect of human connection, it is a powerful vehicle for accomplishing one's purposes. And so it can be distorted by temptations, especially to ambition. Only a robust understanding of holiness, respect and love can keep us from misusing hospitality.

The biblical and historical tradition challenges us to resist cynicism. It is easy to become increasingly callous to brokenness and need. We must help one another with this. We all need to vent at times, but we must also find people who will help us to stay faithful. It is easy to grow grudging in ministry, in hospitality, in providing care, and this is not a new problem. The early Christians struggled too. And every practitioner is challenged in this area. Those who succumb to callousness and cynicism shrivel up, and their work often becomes destructive.

A number of years ago, I worked with my local church in resettling refugees – it turned out to be a massive undertaking. Our congregation of about one hundred and fifty members resettled four hundred refugees in a fairly short period. Life was a combination of wonder and craziness; we got used, hardened and burned out, and it was the best time of our individual and communal lives. We teetered on the edge of cynicism and it became worse when we were terribly tired. Under the constant pressure of unrelenting human need, we were not careful to nourish our lives – and we became very vulnerable. It was a painful but important reality that when we grew weary and when we were used, it was very easy to distance ourselves and to become cynical in order to avoid additional hurt and disappointment.

Practitioners who have gone before us remind us that we must be careful to nourish our lives with prayer, community and Scripture. In the context of suffering, inadequate resources, disappointments, betrayals and sometimes bad choices, we must find adequate sustenance. One woman from the Catholic Worker said that she would never be able to face the 'daily parade of human suffering' were it not for how she was fed in the daily worship service and Eucharist. It is so important to keep a tender heart, looking to Jesus, letting his love and wisdom hold and sustain us. Our own woundedness often surfaces as we work with those in troubled circumstances. We need to be careful to locate ourselves in a community of Christians. We must not look for a perfect community, but for one that wants to be faithful and that challenges us to grow in the image of Christ, to grow in wholeness and holiness.

It is also helpful to locate our work within the larger Christian tradition. As we learn about hospitality and read the Scriptures through the lens of hospitality, we can allow them to shape our thinking about the work we do. It helps to see our work as part of a centuries-old commitment to loving in the hard places and to remember that the small pieces of our jobs fit into a whole way of life that has a rich story. I have come to realise how important this is for faithful practitioners. After I finished teaching a seminar on hospitality, a Salvation Army officer came up to me and said, 'You mean all those beds-and-breakfasts mean something?' He knew they meant something to the recipients, but he had never located his work in the long history of care and hospitality that started with the Old Testament and moved through Christian history and that reflected Jesus' practices and commitments. And he certainly did not know how much his very mundane activities had been part of congregational life in past generations.

The tradition reminds us that hospitality is a strange mixture of very ordinary acts of caring and the promise of God's presence within such acts. Hospitality is full of surprise and mystery. In fact, where else can we find such a combination of pots of soup and 'conversations with angels'? Anyone who has been engaged in a substantial amount of offering welcome knows about this remarkable combination – you know how exhausting the work can be, how crazy the interactions, how unpredictable and how wonderful. You know about the unanticipated blessing, about the needy person you welcome who turns out to be someone who blesses you. When I've talked with practitioners of hospitality, with people who offer hospitality day in and day out, especially to needy people, the most frequently recurring refrain I hear is, 'I went into this ministry thinking that I was helping them, but you know, I've gotten so much more than I've given'. Such outcomes can only be the work of God's grace.

Hospitality helps us to think differently about the nature of the Christian life itself. It helps us see that our discipleship is not first about a series of tasks or duties but rather about a relationship with the living God, a relationship that is full of wonder and mystery because it is lived in response to God's welcome to us.

Conclusion
There are a few more reasons why a recovery of hospitality is important today, especially for those we might identify as the most vulnerable. People who are marginalised by their society are vulnerable in terrible ways and finding welcome can be a move toward recognition and inclusion. Who gets marginalised is culture specific, but in our results-oriented, youth-focused societies, it is the elderly and people with disabilities, recently landed refugees and immigrants, homeless people, troubled teens and unborn children that are often

the marginalised. It's not just that their cries for help are frequently unheard, it's that their gifts and potential contributions are overlooked. Society finds it difficult to imagine that such people could be valuable or interesting, and often the people themselves doubt they have anything to offer.

Central to a recovery of hospitality is recognition of the significance of friendship in the transformation of those who have been marginalised. Hospitality is about close, face-to-face interaction, sharing ourselves and our lives as well as our resources. It is this depth of sharing that is an often-overlooked component of transformation and healing. Especially for those whose lives have been broken, whose relationships have been severed, whose sense of self, purpose and power have been crushed, the experience of being welcomed helps to restore life and hope. People respond when they are given attention and we pay attention to the people we value. In environments where food, shelter and companionship are interrelated, weary and lonely persons can be restored to life. Jean Vanier writes that when people sense 'that they are wanted and loved as they are and that they have a place, then we witness a real transformation – I would say even "resurrection"'.[14]

Years ago, John Cogley described the restoration of persons he witnessed in a Catholic Worker House of Hospitality:

> The security of the House, poor as it was, regular meals, a sure place to sleep, work to be done, the knowledge of being useful to others (…) and the casual but very real fellowship of (…) the place – these things were enough. It was often as if you could see a change taking place before your eyes, like something visible happening – colour returning to a face after a faint.

He went on to observe, 'even the crudest hospitality can work miracles'.[15]

It is hard to imagine what might happen if we became ever more mindful of the significance of welcome. What would happen if we regularly asked ourselves, our congregations and our communities: Who are the invisible people in my world? Who needs welcome? Who needs to know that they are precious to God and to God's people? Whose absence is keeping me, my family and my community from being whole? Are there neighbourhood children, immigrants or migrant workers, single parents, elderly neighbours, foreign students and people with disabilities that we need as part of our community?

Today, just as in centuries past, the practice of hospitality is crucial for the credibility of the Gospel. Robert Webber, author of *Ancient-Future Faith* (1999), writes that for this generation, it is loving communities rather than rational arguments that are persuasive. He suggests that a community that embodies the experience of the kingdom will draw people to itself. 'In this sense, the Church and its life in the world will become the new apologetic. People come to Christian faith not because they see the logic of the argument, but because they have experienced a welcoming God in a hospitable and loving community.'[16]

And finally, today, many people in our societies are open to mystery. They know that life has to consist in more than what they can see or buy or earn. They are looking for meaning and for encounters with God. Sometimes they look in very unhelpful places, but Christians have the mystery, wonder, story and practices that together meet the yearnings for community and meaning and transcendence, yearnings to be helpful to others and to find personal healing in the process. The practice of hospitality is a window into some of the mystery and grace that is central to the life-giving Gospel of Christ.

Notes

1. See Christine D. Pohl, *Making Room: Recovering Hospitality as a Christian Tradition*, Grand Rapids, Mich: Wm. B. Eerdmans, 1999.
2. Krister Stendahl, 'When you pray, pray in this manner ...' A Bible Study in *The Kingdom on Its Way: Meditations and Music for Mission*, RISK Book Series (Geneva: World Council of Churches, 1980), pp. 40–41, quoted

in Letty Russell, *Household of Freedom,* Philadelphia: Westminster, 1987, p. 76.

3. All biblical quotations are taken from the *The Holy Bible, New Revised Standard Version.*

4. See Deuteronomy 24:14-15, 17-22.

5. Mother Teresa, quoted in Eileen Egan, 'Dorothy Day, Pilgrim of Peace' in *A Revolution of the Heart: Essays on the Catholic Worker,* ed. Patrick G. Coy, Philadelphia: Temple University Press, 1988, p. 105.

6. 'First Apology of Justin', ch. 14, *The Ante-Nicene Fathers,* Edinburgh: T. & T. Clark, 1867-72, Vol. 1, p. 167.

7. Ibid., ch. 67, p. 186.

8. Lactantius, *The Divine Institutes,* book 6, chapter 12, *The Ante-Nicene Fathers,* Vol. 7, p. 176.

9. Ibid., pp. 176–177.

10. John Chrysostom, Homily 45 on Acts, *Nicene and Post-Nicene Fathers, Series 1,* Vol. 11, p. 276, and Homily 14 on 1 Timothy, *NPNF1,* Vol. 13, p. 455.

11. John Chrysostom, Homily 41 on Genesis, in *Homilies on Genesis 18-45,* trans. Robert C. Hill, *The Fathers of the Church,* Vol. 82, Washington, D.C.: Catholic University of America Press, 1990, p. 413.

12. Philip Hallie, *Tales of Good and Evil, Help and Harm,* New York: HarperCollins, 1997, p. 207.

13. John Calvin, *Sermons from Job,* Grand Rapids, Mich.: Wm. B. Eerdmans, 1952, pp. 202, 204–206.

14. Jean Vanier, *From Brokenness to Community,* New York: Paulist Press, 1992, p. 15.

15. John Cogley, 'House of Hospitality,' October 1947, in *A Penny a Copy: Readings from 'The Catholic Worker',* ed. Thomas C. Cornell, Robert Ellsberg and Jim Forest, Maryknoll, N.Y.: Orbis Books, 1995, p. 56.

16. Robert E. Webber, *Ancient-Future Faith: Rethinking Evangelicalism for a Postmodern World,* Michigan: Baker Academic, 1999.

Towards a Poetics of Hospitality

John O'Donohue

In this chapter I intend to explore some of the implicit philosophy behind the notion of strangeness, the stranger and the idea of hospitality with a view to grounding a creative and critical poetics of hospitality. I would like to begin with a poem I wrote several years ago called 'Beannacht'. In a sense, a blessing is a form of invocation which unites welcome, recognition and generosity in the face of potential strangeness.

Beannacht
On the day when
The weight deadens
On your shoulders
And you stumble,
May the clay dance
To balance you.

And when your eyes
Freeze behind the grey window
And the ghost of loss
Gets into you,
May a flock of colours,
Indigo, red, green
And azure blue
Come to awaken in you
A meadow of delight.

When the canvas frays
In the currach of thought
And the stain of ocean

Blackens beneath you,
May there come across the waters
A path of yellow moonlight
To bring you safely home.

May the nourishment of the earth be yours.
May the clarity of light be yours.
May the fluency of the ocean be yours.
May the protection of the ancestors be yours.

And so may a slow
Wind work these words
Of love around you,
An invisible cloak
To mind your life.

Strangeness is difficult to describe because it is always exceptional and unusual. And why is this so? It is so because the familiarity of our world becomes fixed, rigidified and complacent. Hegel said in the *Phenomenology of Spirit* that 'the familiar, precisely because it is familiar, remains unknown'. Who knows what hides beneath the familiar? That is what artists are always after. If you are in the obsessive business of trying to find words for the whispers you hear in your heart, then what you are doing is excavating the lineaments of the ordinary to find what is strangely there. We constantly take experience to be solid. And in a sense, it is. Once your body is in the world, you are heir to an endless plenitude and abundance. Yet, the great French philosopher, Albert Camus, an expert on strangeness, said that after one day in the world you could spend the rest of your life in solitary confinement and you would still have something to be unpacking or unfolding. Even within the most commonplace experience, strangeness remains but a light sleeper.

The Strain of the Ordinary

That is the mystery of mornings. Mornings are amazing places. We return to the world we abandoned last night to find that it is still there, intact, awaiting us, and we return as the selves who had voyaged off into the night. It is a real achievement to come through to morning. Imagine a short story about somebody who got stranded in the night and never actually made it through into the morning. In the morning, everything begins again. This links in with the medieval philosophical notion of *concursus*, i.e. the idea that God sustains the simultaneity of creation at every moment.

The continual and subtle sustaining of the world in our view and presence is miraculous. It is very difficult for us to see the world anew because we find ourselves at the present endpoint of evolution, and evolution has a huge drive towards domestication. We tire of the nomadic; we want to settle. We rest in the familiar, the complacent and in our own private and institutional membership of different idolatrous systems. It is what Marx would call 'alienation'. Then our thought begins to resemble our chosen mode of complacency. We immunise ourselves against what might be strange or disturbing.

Plato said in the *Timaeus* that all thought begins with rupture, with the recognition that something is out of place. This is what strangeness is. Because we are so woven into the fabric of familiarity, strangeness has to be exceptional for us. Yet it can rupture; it can arise at any moment. For instance, when you are in the middle of your life, you have fifty things to do and the phone rings. You pick it up and you get news that somebody you love is very seriously ill and could die within the next hour. It takes three seconds to communicate that information, but when you put the phone down, you are already standing in a different world. That is all it takes for you to be expelled from the familiarity of your world and exposed to the raw contingency of total strangeness. To put it poetically: even mountains are suspended on strings.

Perhaps a sign of awakening and spiritual maturity is to begin a friendship with strangeness that it might become a constant, challenging, creative companion to your perception, imagination and feeling. This is another way to transform your death, because ultimately the fear of death is grounded in the stranger that will come at the end to expel you. But death need not be a stranger if your life has not shied from its subtle yet pervasive presence.

The Dimensions of Strangeness

There are different dimensions to the notion of the stranger and strangeness. One of the first stages in all perception and knowing is the recognition of difference. When we arrive in the world, we learn sameness. There is the surface sameness, where things are the same day in and day out, though we never know what may be happening in the quietness below the surface. In contrast, there are things that are different. Looking at our hospitality towards difference, it is interesting to ask ourselves: Where do we draw our contours of exclusion and complacency? And how do we hold to them? Frequently, the times of greatest growth are the times when we have the courage to open ourselves to difference.

More intense yet is the notion of othernesss. Otherness is difference that you cannot immediately domesticate or assimilate. Then there is the presence of that which is strange. Etymologically, the word 'strange' was originally defined spatially. That was strange which was 'extraneous and outside'; 'that is strange which does not originate where it is found'. The notion of the 'unknown' is suggested there. In the Oxford English Dictionary 'strange' also stood as the omen for what was completely different. A tealeaf appearing on top of the surface could indicate a stranger. At home, when we would be at dinner, if a knife fell off the table, my mother would say there were strangers coming. Or if sparks fell out of the grate, she would say there was money coming. In other places, if a stranger came on a Monday, an invasion of strangers might continue for the week.

The most intense level of difference is that which is alien, what the Germans call *das Fremde*, that which is so completely other that your points of continuity with it are almost non-existent. One of the most fascinating questions, of course, in philosophy, and in the philosophy of language particularly, is that it is not even possible to conceive of that which is totally strange. You cannot even imagine it because the reflexivity of language catches you all the time; but that is a whole other question.

Who is the Stranger?

Who is the stranger? The simple answer is, 'I am the stranger'. We forget that our first identity is as stranger. We forget that we turn up on the planet as complete strangers. When your mother was pregnant, no one knew who you would be or what you might look like. Your arrival into identity was primitive; you were a complete stranger. Doris Lessing, in her disturbing novel *The Fifth Child*, explores the danger of birth as total intrusion. It portrays a family of four children full of love until the arrival of the fifth … Therefore, each of us is the stranger and we come into the world in that strange way. Indeed, Jesus did the same thing. I want to read this sonnet that I wrote on the Nativity:

The Nativity
No man reaches where the moon touches a woman.
Even the moon leaves her when she opens
Deeper into the ripple in her womb
That encircles dark to become flesh and bone.

Someone is coming ashore inside her.
A face deciphers itself from water
And she curves around the gathering wave,
Opening to offer the life it craves.

In a corner stall of pilgrim strangers,
She falls and heaves, holding a tide of tears.
A red wire of pain feeds through every vein
Until night unweaves and the child reaches dawn.

Outside each other, now, she sees him first.
Flesh of her flesh, her dreamt son safe on earth.

Originally, each one of us is the stranger. It belongs to the incredible subtlety of our facility for domestication that we are almost totally amnesiac about where we have come from. People seem to speak readily of what the future holds and maybe what happened last week, but seldom does the conversation reach back to the primary source where somebody asks: 'I wonder where we were before we got here at all?' My purpose in outlining the repressed yet native strangeness of being here is to underline how exceptional normality and familiarity actually are.

The Surrounding Strangeness

It is strange all around. A simple illustration of this is to notice what happens to you when you enter the world of dream. Perfectly respectable, mature, even shadowless people are up to the most amazing things at night in their dreams. That they manage to show up for breakfast, appearing normal, is a huge achievement. Inside your body it is also completely dark and all your thinking is born in darkness. Furthermore, all of your journeys are from the unknown and from the dark out towards the light. Even the earth itself has no cover, no shelter. At night, you look up, out into the millions of light years of distance. No wonder Pascal said, 'The silence of these infinite spaces terrifies me'.

The landscape of otherness becomes even more intricate and intense when you consider the microcosmic world of matter. A little splinter of timber or a small stone actually holds geographies, continents within it. Imagine how microcosmic travel through it could take hundreds of thousands of years. It is surely one of our blindest and most convenient human acts to consider that world as inanimate. The opposite is patently true. Matter is magnificently intense and alive in all its oblique and subtle gyrations.

Indeed, when you consider your own acquaintances and friends and all the mystery that grounds and surrounds that, the wonder is that we are able to negotiate the otherness at all and achieve such levels of pure intimacy. Perhaps the psychological heart of our difficulty with strangeness and strangers issues from the fact that we are made uneasy by what is foreign and different because we have not made peace with it within. A profitable exercise to do sometimes in meditation, or even in writing, is to imagine coming upon yourself as a total stranger.

Sometimes an unusual question brings the latent surrounding strangeness to the surface: 'Is there this evening a stranger whom you have never met and never will meet, who is walking home through the streets of Leningrad, but whose life has had an incredible influence on yours?' It could be so. Who knows how the script of otherness is structured: why we encounter the styles of otherness that we do, why we find it easier to engage with some and reject others and why some styles of otherness never come within the orbit of our journey?

The Denial of Interior Strangeness

Derek Walcott has a beautiful poem, 'Love After Love', which illustrates the desire and dream of hospitality towards one's own neglected strangeness and intimacy:

Love after Love
The time will come
When, with elation,
You will greet yourself arriving
At your own door, in your own mirror,
And each will smile at the other's welcome,

And say sit here. Eat.
You will love again the stranger who was yourself.
Give wine. Give bread. Give back your heart
To itself, to the stranger who has loved you

All your life, whom you ignored
For another, who knows you by heart.
Take down the old love letters from the bookshelf,

The photographs, the desperate notes,
Peel your own image from the mirror.
Sit. Feast on your life.

A crucial dimension of the human journey is to develop a worthy, critical, forgiving and truly adventurous friendship with the stranger that you are; this entails respect for your own otherness, viz. not to squander your precious strangeness or sell it off cheaply to second-hand spiritual or psychological programmes. The challenge is to remain faithful to it because it was chosen for you since that primal time when your essence was first dreamed.

The other forgotten aspect of this theme is that human identity is in fact pitched between two regions of strangeness: the unknown of our origin and the incredible strangeness that yet awaits each of us. This is not just romantic philosophy. A pure otherness will come to end our lives, the strangeness of death. Death is the ultimate stranger. Perhaps the secret to the transfiguration of one's death is to allow the stranger to be your companion so that at the end when he beckons you to depart, you will be voyaging with a well known friend and not with a presence that is forcing you into some eternal exile.

The Strangeness of God

The last aspect of strangeness that I want to mention is God as stranger. The tendency in all religion is to become ideology and to domesticate God into some fashionable institutional icon. The duty of theology is to remain vigilant and constantly fight ideology, to keep the divine sacred, free and dangerous. The people who keep best vigilance are the mystics. The person whose work in this area I admire most is Meister Eckhart, a fourteenth century mystic. In mystical theology, he fashioned in one phrase his most devastating insight; it is in middle high German and says: *Gott wirt und Gott entwirt* – 'God becomes and God unbecomes'. This is the ultimate faithfulness to God as stranger. It says that God is only our name for it and the closer we come to it, the more it ceases to be God. This recognition reaches across the centuries to qualify and even tame the vehemence of Hegel and the Death of God theology. Eckhart has penetrated more deeply into the terrifying otherness of the Divine. At the heart of the Christian tradition there is an indissoluble unity between the total stranger and the all-embracing intimacy, which is incarnated and deepened even further in the Eucharist.

Towards a Phenomenology of the Stranger

What is suggesting itself here is a possible phenomenology of the stranger. The stranger is not a neutral presence. Firstly, the emergence of the stranger is usually an irruption or interruption. The stranger arrives. When we were children, people in our valley rarely travelled. There was the usual trip to town, but outside of that a visit to the city was a major event. When we saw people coming, we would say, 'There are strangers coming'. Secondly, the stranger was a surprise. And there is a gift in the stranger. However, this can be deeply ambivalent because the stranger can also be dangerous and destructive. It behoves one who is a custodian of the gateways through which the stranger comes to exercise discernment.

Recently, I discussed this question with a friend who runs a spiritual community that is open to taking on strangers to come and live with them for a period, participating in their communal life. He said: 'In the beginning we had some visitors who were quite destructive, but that was due to our own ignorance and blindness. Now we have a more subtle process of discernment and we can say to somebody, "We think it would be better for you and better for us if you tried somewhere else".' Thirdly, the stranger often brings an invitation to go on a new journey of knowing, pushing the old frontiers.

Initially, the stranger can appear under the mask of caricature. He is unknown and dwells deep within the outer image that he projects and is projected on to him. This can be an awkward and difficult journey from image to presence. This is the heart of the whole question of hospitality and generosity to the stranger. It is all about the transfiguration of anonymity into intimacy and presence. Because that is what we all long for: real presence.

When Presence becomes Real, Anything can Happen!
Some years ago on a German TV programme called *Wortwechsel*, I heard a wonderful story that illustrates perfectly the potential of real presence. It was an interview with the Hungarian novelist, Gyorky Konrad. He is an old man now and one of the most famous Hungarian novelists. He told the story of when he was a child of eight and his little sister was about six. One weekend his parents went on a trip out of the country and that happened to be the weekend that Hitler invaded Hungary. The borders were closed. The two children were trapped inside and the parents were outside and could not return. But he was an astute child and he investigated the possibilities until he heard that there was a lawyer who took people across the border. He went to him and said, 'My sister and I need to get out'. The lawyer said, 'It will cost you a lot of money', to which the young Konrad replied, 'I know where the family money is'. The lawyer asked how much he had and he foolishly told the lawyer, who said, 'That's what it will cost you'. The child gave him all the money.

One evening the lawyer brought them towards the border. They were just coming to the border when they were surrounded by a platoon of German soldiers. The captain sent the lawyer scurrying back home and appointed one of his young soldiers to take the two children aside and shoot them. The soldier brought the two children over to a tree and raised his rifle. First he aimed at the little boy and the little boy, now telling the story as an old man, said: 'My eyes opened in absolute amazement that one human being could do this to another. Something in my look caught the soldier's eyes and our gazes locked. And for the longest time they held, and then gradually, he lowered his rifle and sent us across the border.'

What happened in that story was real presence. The true presence of the little child, the gaze, cut through all the layers of indoctrination in this killer, recalling him to his humanity, and the moment he became human again he could no longer kill. This is what real presence is all about.

The Fatal Domestication of Otherness

In post-modern culture, one of the great difficulties is otherness. This is a huge philosophical question. Otherness becomes intense at an existential level between people when it has been erased from their surrounding life. I heard the physicist Brian Swimme say in California, a few years ago, that we are one of the first generations that have managed to forget that we live in a universe. It is truly disturbing to think that many people now participate more fully as citizens of cyberspace than of actual earth space. Peter Sloterdyk, the Austrian critic, said: 'The computer world is full of foreground but it has no background.' This relates to the power and force of media as one of the supreme homogenising agents in the world. The images and the sound bites are nearly all the same and they span the whole world.

If the normal sources of unfiltered otherness and difference are not being frequently encountered, but replaced by ersatz versions, when we meet real otherness, it evokes a sense of threat and panic. If otherness has to do with presence, then it has to do simply with human identity, and with the integrity, complexity, danger and limitation of the other self. At its heart, this is not about process. It is not about procedures and it is not about structures. It is about the simple fact of one human person standing in front of another and recognising that they are being faced by a world that is autonomous and over which they have no control or power. Yet no one stands alone as an island of pure, unreachable otherness. Perception, language and intention furnish us with a whole set of subtle bridges that are already being crossed the first moment the encounter begins. To discern the gifts and challenges then becomes the challenge and the adventure.

Creative Duality and Imagination

In the western philosophical and spiritual tradition, one of the dimensions that has been radically neglected is imagination. This neglect of the imagination and the preferment of will working together with naked intellect has yielded such a sad harvest of division and separation for the western Christian psyche. There is a natural duality that runs right through experience: inside / outside, time/eternity, darkness/light, self/other, divine/human, eros/mind, masculine/feminine. The difficulty arises when the dualistic mind engages with duality. The frontiers where dualities meet become frozen and one side becomes separated from the other. This division proves destructive. One side assumes a false dominance, and from its one-dimensional perspective it proceeds to repress its other side which is then caricatured as a threat and a danger. This is the epistemological perspective which accounts for the scapegoating and demonisation of the stranger as carrier of suspicion and threat. This in turn leads to the exclusion and exile of the stranger. The resolution and integration of such falsely manufactured otherness is slow and difficult work. It can only begin when there is generous openness to real conversation and recognition. Then, the false borders begin to fall and the retrieval of the other in affinity can lead to the recovery of one's own banished otherness and the integration of self and other. Here again the imagination is the key faculty that can begin to lift the false image from the other and allow his countenance to appear.

Violence and the Failure of Imagination

To my mind, the human faculty most excited by that conversation, most drawn to it, and most capable of nourishing it with the hospitality that allows full voice to both sides, is the imagination. The imagination is committed to the justice of wholesomeness. And all acts of violence against people who are different begin in the imagination, or rather with the failure of imagination. This often struck me in relation to Northern Ireland. How is it possible for someone to walk into a house and kill a father who is sitting down with his wife and children? The only way that is possible is through a prior process of caricature and demonisation through which the other no longer remains a person but has become a thing of horror. Yet if the killer could say at that moment, 'My God, his little girl is wearing something that I just bought for my daughter last week', he would never be able to pull the trigger. Most difficulty in relation to otherness and in relation to those who are very different from us has to do with frozen or failed imagination. True leadership in this regard is about awakening the imagination and allowing oneself to stand for a little while imaginatively in the shoes of that other person.

Hospitality has a Different Logic

This is exactly where the beauty of hospitality can become subversive, because hospitality has its own logic, which runs counter to the kind of marketing and functional logic of contemporary society. An epistemology of quantity governs much of contemporary life. It is allied to a logic of exponential multiplication. We become addicted and frenetic; desire becomes swollen to want more and more and more. This is driven by the inner deity that choreographs most of contemporary culture, viz. the market. We live in a time of what the writer and visionary politician Michael D. Higgins calls 'market fundamentalism'. This is evident, for instance, in the presentation of Ireland to Ireland and Ireland to the outside; all of this is done now, almost exclusively, in marketing terms. It is fascinating how unconsciously this language takes over. Hospitality is a different thing because it is attuned to the logic of the invisible and it gives, not wanting a return.

This is how the law of spirit differs from the law of matter. According to the law of matter, if I have one piece and I get four more, then I have five. However, according to the law of spirit, less can be more. It is the inverse proportion, and that is why in the law of spirit absence and emptiness are often the greatest wells of fecundity. Generosity is its own reward and hospitality also has that willingness to go the extra mile.

The experience of receiving hospitality is hugely instructive of a different way of being; there is a certain decorum and graciousness in it which is not personal. I do not mean it is not personal in the sense that it is impersonal but rather that it is not self-referential: 'See what an incredible host I am that I am doing this for you.' No, it is serving an unseen dignity in you, in the host and in the event of your being together. In a certain sense, hospitality is the secret priesthood, or priestliness, of real presence.

Honour and Hospitality in the Irish Tradition

In the old Irish tradition, there were amazing dimensions to hospitality. Even now the introduction-anthem to Ireland is 'Céad Mile Fáilte'. In ancient battle, one might fight all day long with an enemy, but at evening the strictures of hospitality were rigorously observed, though the following morning would see the battle continue. If one was in conflict with someone and they happened to arrive at one's dwelling, regardless of the conflict, on arrival they were offered a meal and hospitality.

In the monastic tradition, when a guest came in they recieved three things: a good meal, their feet were washed and they got a fresh bed of straw and a candle. And if they arrived in the monastery where a fast was already being observed, the Abbot called off the fast and there was a celebration of the guest. The arrival of the stranger was an event that caused the suspension of the normal daily round. It must be remembered that in folk culture, when a stranger arrived, the content of the visit would resemble several nights of our intense radio, television or cinema, because so few travelled then. The stranger was exciting because he brought news from everywhere.

The whole notion of honour was central in the ancient Irish tradition. The king, the bishop and the poet enjoyed huge honour. If you belonged to a lower social level and felt the king had been unfair to you, you could fast against him. But you had to fast where everyone could see you. You would fast outside the door. Then the rule was that the king inside had to fast as well, then the next day he would come out and talk to you and arbitrate; and if he ignored you, he incurred a huge loss of face. It is very interesting to note how the strictures of hospitality held the decorum of society together. This decorum of hospitality was also a means of achieving justice, of restoring the balance that had been violated.

The Human Face: Call and Confirmation

There is an ironic sense in which the rubric of hospitality and interaction is grounded metaphorically in the image of the human face. The human face is the icon of creation. It is the arrival point where all the anonymity of the universe is transformed into intimacy. And I imagine that when the human face first appeared on earth, the winds went silent and the waves were stilled by what had actually arrived.

It is quite amazing to have a face. And what is more amazing still is that you have never seen your own face. All you have seen is the image of your face in a mirror. And mirrors are notoriously fickle; some are overly kind and some can be quite sadistic. Therefore, in a certain sense, the actual validation of who you are requires the gaze of the other. We are only partly there and we need each other to know and to feel that we are fully there. The human face is actually the face of others. We are masterpieces of a divine imagination that made us for each other; we incarnate and express this in the very structures of our physiology. But it is also mirrored internally. There is in each of us that incommensurable place where we can be reached by nothing other than the Divine. The face of the other is a call to recognition and hospitality. It is also the call to the other to confirm me and return me to myself. In the gaze of the other I return home. In the African tradition, there is the fascinating notion of *Ubuntu* – on my own I am no one. Only through others can I become myself.

Emmanuel Levinas: The Face as Subversive Presence and Invitation

The French philosopher, Emmanuel Levinas, has very interesting insights into this whole thematic. Though radically influenced by both Husserl and Heidegger, he distinguishes himself from them in his absolute concentration on the face of the human individual. Heidegger's claim was that Being has been forgotten in the western tradition. But Levinas argues that in the methodology Heidegger employs to retrieve Being, he ends up reducing everything to its modalities of being. The beauty of Husserl is his discovery of the magic and creativity of consciousness through his focus on the intentional power of consciousness. And Levinas too shares this perspective but continues to insist that the face signifies the resistance of the other to our power and possessiveness. The face achieves this through its reference to itself which is its own identity, to which I can have no claim or access.

Levinas speaks then about the notion of thought as connecting us. Because the other being is a totality in itself, how can I get that totality inside myself? He claims this can be achieved through the miracle of thinking. Thinking is the discovery of the other and the taking in of the other into my world. For him, interiority and memory reverse historical time, thus offering ever-new possibilities of presence. Central here is the role of language as transformation. It is in and through language that the bridges between us are actually laid down. Yet Levinas insists throughout of the inviolability, irreducibility and complete otherness of the human face that faces me. He says: 'I don't break any system or cause a rupture in it; it is the human face that no language, concept or system, can actually claim.' It would be very interesting theologically to take his idea and look at the theology of icons in the orthodox tradition. This line of thinking could be used further to ground and articulate the whole spirituality of the Order of St John of God. Your work demands something that subversive and intimate, namely, the image of the human face that resists and indeed subverts any institutional claim to appropriate the native integrity of the person.

The Spirituality of Greed

The question of hospitality necessarily includes reference to the nature and practice of greed. The etymology of the word 'mean' is very interesting. It is that which is common to two or more people, possessed jointly, but it also has meanings like: inferior, poor in quality, undignified, small or muddled. It seems to suggest the violation of dignity. This etymological line could be amplified in an analysis of greed through invoking Freudian psychology; this could illuminate some of the dimensions of greed in our culture, understood namely as a fixation and paralysis at the oral stage. There is some kind of regression at work here. Greed is also, of course, the corruption of desire. There is nothing as beautiful as desire and longing. What is ruining so much of the resources of the world and absolutely turning the hearts of some humans into deserts is greed as corrupted desire. The loneliness of greed is that no matter how successful you are at it you can never find ease within its contour; it offers no shelter, only frenzy. The logic of 'never enough' means that you will never be able to enjoy what you actually have. To succumb to greed is to paralyse one's capacity for recognition and celebration.

The Eucharist: What is Alien becomes Intimate

I want to conclude with a consideration of the Eucharist. I think that the Eucharist is one of the most amazing windows in the whole of creation. It is the transfiguration of the most sublime and subversive strangeness, namely, the horror of crucifixion into the birth and beginning of new life. That is the axis that is active at the heart of the Eucharist. In some strange way, sacramental time does not happen only in historical time. There is a profound sense in when the Eucharist is celebrated; it is all in the now of the then that was. Through the communion of saints and the participation in the body of Christ, we slip into the eternal rhythm from which historical time derives its current and form.

The absolute desolation of the pain of the world creeps inside the bread. The pain of those who were/are present and those who are/were absent and those who are/were unseen are within it as well. The amazing thing about the Eucharist is that no difference is dark enough to be left outside. It is the circle which includes all 'that is' and all 'that is not'. It includes all possibility and impossibility, all that was, is and will be. The whole Eucharist turns on the imagination of Jesus. If Jesus had had no imagination, we would know nothing about the Incarnation. How would we know? It was the imagination of Jesus that helped him to realise where he was from and who he was. That was an amazing opening. To link the Incarnation existentially with the stranger in our world, the otherness within the self and with the strangeness that is death, that is a conversation that needs to happen existentially. In a certain ontological sense that is exactly the conversation that is already and always happening through all of us at the heart of the Eucharist. The Eucharist might be said in one place but it is said in no place because it is everywhere; it issues from a simultaneity that can never be broken.

There is huge nourishment here. The Eucharist is the source and the summit of all hospitality. This is the profound irony of Jesus. He was the outsider, a refugee, but in actual fact, ontologically, he was the total insider. He issued from within the very birth-source of the primal and proximate narrative of what is. Then he turns up as an outsider to come back in again in a realised way, right into the heart of the whole thing, an incredible narrative that is at once utter drama and utter stillness.

Beholding the Stranger in our Midst

A Conversation with John Hull[1]

The following is a transcript of a discussion between Professor John Hull and Andrew McGrady which explores the notion of the Christian response to 'the stranger in our midst' through the lens of John Hull's personal experience of blindness. It draws upon a number of presentations that John has made concerning the spirituality of disability and its implications for the charism of hospitality.

Andrew McGrady: John, is the person who is blinded a 'stranger in our midst'?

John Hull: There is little doubt that disabled people encounter some difficulties in church life. I do not suppose these are any more pronounced than one finds in the secular world as a whole, but on the other hand, perhaps there are certain features worth mentioning. It is noticeable that the Church lags behind the human rights agenda in the areas of non-discrimination for people of various sexual orientations, and in the equal participation of men and women in public life and ministry. This is also the case with disability. In the UK, for instance, many Churches are now hastily trying to conform to the requirements of the Disability Discrimination Act, having previously paid but little attention to this issue. The time lag, if that is what accounts for it, is presumably the consequence of the shadows of prejudice that have been carried over from the ancient world in which Christian faith originated, and a natural conservatism has made the Churches reluctant to discard even those elements of the tradition that are now seriously out of date, both socially and ethically. This is bringing the Church, and indeed Christian faith itself, into disrepute with many disabled people who will often remark that the Church is not part of the answer but part of the problem.

It might be thought that the stories of the miraculous healing of disabled people, particularly those attributed to Jesus, and the history of the Churches' care and protection for disabled people, would have inspired a more positive evaluation but the situation is more complicated. Certainly, there has been considerable compassion towards disabled people, but people today do not want compassion; rather, they want the full exercise of their human rights, equality of opportunity and a reasonable level of economic life. To put it rather bluntly, 'compassion' – or as it is sometimes experienced, 'pity' – is degrading, and one of the problems that many disabled people find in Christian communities is what we might call the 'surplus of compassion'. This is the replacement of Christian justice by Christian love.

As for the miracles of Jesus, some disabled people find these stories rather embarrassing, since the implication is that if they had a bit more faith, they would be healed. The invitation to miraculous healing is felt by some disabled people as a rather humiliating offer. The assumption is that they are not healed, that curing is the same as healing and that they are longing for some other life than the one they live. For many disabled people, being disabled is not a problem, because there is nothing that can be done about it. What is a problem is getting into the church in a wheelchair – getting over the step.

This brings us to the distinction between impairment and disability, a distinction that is at the heart of the modern disability rights movement. You are impaired when part of your body, or an aspect of body or mind, is not functioning properly. Impairment is dealt with by medical intervention and often by technology. Disability is a social concept. One is disabled when access is denied because of preventable conditions. If I lose my legs, I become impaired; my mobility can be largely restored by a modern wheelchair. But as I roll along on my way to a meeting, it is the stairs that disable me. Disability is to be countered by education, and by social reform.

I have a friend who is training for the ordained ministry. Some years ago, as a consequence of an illness, her toes had to be surgically removed. At first confined to a wheelchair, she gradually learned to walk again, and today mobility is not a problem for her. However, she also lost several fingers. She lives a normal life, and has been employed successfully for several years. She does not think of herself as disabled, but as impaired. Now that she contemplates using her hands in very public contexts, she is aware of the possibility that she might drop her sermon notes, fumble in turning the pages of the Bible or hymn book, and even worse, might drop the chalice. She could so easily be disabled by an officious priest standing beside her and telling her that she better not take any risks. She hopes to remain only impaired, and not be disabled by the Church.

Behind all such attitudes lies the ideal of a single converging perfection, and all that this implies for people whose bodies, and perhaps minds, are not similar to what is normally considered to be perfect. But to unravel that would take us into another discussion.

AMG: Given the centrality of 'compassion' within the three Abrahamic faiths (Christianity, Judaism, Islam) and the Eastern religions (for instance, Buddhism), your comment concerning a 'surplus of compassion' seems rather strong. For example, did not Jesus describe the Good Samaritan as being 'moved with compassion' when he saw the half-dead man on the Jericho road (Lk 10:33 [JB]). Is not compassion essentially an active solidarity based upon the recognition of a common humanity?

JH: You have asked me about the character of compassion when extended towards people living with disabilities. Generally, people with disabilities, like anyone else, enjoy autonomy and seek as far as possible to live independent lives. There are some impaired people who are disabled by the fears of their families, and lose all independence, becoming institutionalised in disability, passive, and eventually losing much interest in life. I have heard, for instance, of a blind man who never left his house after losing his sight. His family were so worried about him, and he collaborated. The same often happens with the parents of children with disabilities. They surround their child with loving care, wrapping them up in cotton wool, as we say, so that the child fails to develop a confident, vigorous approach to life. This is related to the vexed problem of how to help people living with disabilities. Generally speaking, my rule is to advise people not to offer help until it is requested, and this would apply to everyone, whether disabled or not. Let us suppose you, a person with normal ability, are getting into your car when you hear someone calling out, 'Stop!' There are the sounds of running footsteps, and a stranger appears panting by your side offering help. What would you think? You would probably ask yourself how much of an incompetent fool you looked to evoke such a response! It is the same with disabled people. Here I am approaching the lift. Just as I locate the call buttons with my left hand, and am about to press the correct one with my right hand, some other hand slips under mine and a voice says triumphantly, 'There! I've got it for you!'

Much of this kind of unwanted help springs from a basic misunderstanding about the way that blind people negotiate the world. It reflects the fact that the disabled person is a stranger from the point of view of the majority. Here I am, having crossed the busy road, and moving on my regular route towards the open pedestrian gate of the campus. I cannot risk veering to the right. This might take me out into the line of cars entering the campus through the main gate. So I veer to the left, for safety, and my cane is just about to strike the wall, which I intend to follow round until I come to the gate I want, when someone rushes over and says, 'Stop! You are walking into a wall!' But I am not walking into the wall; I am finding out exactly where it is so that I can follow it. I have to make contact with the fabric in order to do this. The person trying to be helpful simply has no understanding of how a blind person navigates space.

At this point someone always asks about the situation where a blind person is walking directly towards a hole in the road. Well, you must use common sense, just as you would with anyone else. Open holes in the road are dangerous for anyone, and I suppose a sighted person in a hurry might be as likely to fall in as a blind person carefully testing the ground with a white cane. These things are difficult and the answer often depends upon a knowledge of the world of disabilities, plus common sense. My protest is directed towards the common experience of disabled people of being oppressed by unwanted offers of help, every one of which creates a little decline in confidence and self esteem. A friend who uses two crutches told me that as she approaches the altar, having walked down the aisle, she has to carefully remove each crutch and lock it up. She can do this quite easily, and has done so hundreds of times. But now she is surrounded by people wanting to help. She exclaimed, 'If only they would let me alone!' That is what I have in mind when I speak of the surplus of compassion. It is such a relief to be taken for granted.

Now I would like to take this discussion a little deeper. It is healthy and natural for each one of us to feel at home in his or her own world. Anthropologists have developed techniques for entering into the strange world of other cultures, and it is accepted that a thorough and deep insight might take not only months but years. This is the case with entry into a culture which is obviously different from one's own, because of the language, or the skin colour, or the climate. But when we approach a person with a disability in our own culture, one who shares our ethnic identity, skin colour and language, it is easy to overlook the fact that someone who uses a wheelchair may have a different perspective upon the environment, and if we meet a person who uses a linguistic medium other than speech, with whom communication might be difficult, it is all too easy to assume that the other person is stupid. This is often the experience of sign-using deaf people. But this familiarity with our bodies in our own world is inevitable. It is normal. When we meet someone from a different world, we may unconsciously protect our world from challenge by failing to recognise the otherness of the other world. Such an encounter might be disturbing because it might hold up the possibility of losing our own world, the uncomfortable realisation of our own fragility. It is easier to regard the other not as dwelling in a different world, but rather as excluded from our own world, as being world-less. Such a person 'deserves our compassion', for what would it be like to be without a world!

It is this kind of compassion that may be regarded as a tribute to our own world, an instinctive clinging to our own normality and its absolute truth. In that context, compassion may become excessive and a defence against acceptance rather than a genuine encounter.

AMG: Given what you have just said, John, could it not be argued that the person who shows a 'surplus of compassion' in fact shows no compassion at all but rather feels threatened by the strangeness of the 'other' and acts in a way that seeks to maintain the stability of his or her world by insisting the 'stranger' conform to the practices of that world?

JH: I did not argue against compassion itself. I believe that one should have compassion for all living things, and I do not doubt that there are tragic situations both for communities and individuals that rightly evoke a particularly strong feeling of compassion. However, in many of the emotional aspects of life, there is the question of excess. We all expect to receive the respect of other people, but excessive respect can become a kind of insincere deference, which verges upon lack of respect. Consider, for example, the elaborate and emphatic use of the word 'gentleman' towards an unruly drunk who is about to be tossed out of the bar! Another example of over-emphatic emotion is in love. Everyone likes to be told that they are loved, but if piles of flowers suddenly appear on the doorstep, many women might wonder what it's all about. Sigmund Freud has shown us that love and hate are closely linked, that all love contains some hatred, and that one way of expressing hostility is to be excessively loving. Freud described this as 'the return of the repressed'. It means that when an attempt is made to hide one's real feelings under their opposite, the deeper feeling may finally emerge.

This is the kind of theory of the emotions that has caused me to become suspicious of much of the loving care that I, along with other disabled people, tend to receive. I have often wondered why my academic colleagues in the line in front of me waiting for coffee are addressed as 'Dr' so-and-so or 'Professor' such-and-such, but when I get to the front it is 'Love'. Why should I be selected for love above my colleagues? I suspect that it is because my colleagues look business-like, and give a quick glance that anticipates rapid service and no nonsense, but a blind person, who obviously has had to place a finger under someone's elbow in order to retain a place in the line, and then has to touch the counter in order to make sure that it is there, and has to ask what kind of sandwiches are available instead of taking this fact in at a glance appears pathetic and child-like. But, as you suggest in your question, there is the challenge of unfamiliarity, the shock of difference. The blind person might smile in the wrong direction until greeted, cannot be recruited with a smile, is unaware of body language, and so on. To someone used to working and living with blind people, these 'blindisms', as they are sometimes called, are familiar, but to many, they appear strange and maybe frightening. I remember how, forty years ago, a very sensible elderly lady told me that when she was getting onto the train with her case, a kindly porter offered her a hand. He took the handle of her suitcase and his black hand touch her white one, and she told me that she almost dropped the case, it was such a shock. I have been told similar stories by British African priests who have sometimes found that a communicant, kneeling at the rail with hand outstretched for the bread, instantly draws it back when the hand of the priest, holding the paten, comes into view. Such incidents are, I am sure, becoming less common, as people get used to mixing with people from various ethnic backgrounds, but the strangeness of disability still lingers as a threat to normality.

This threat is not only the exposure to a different kind of body, but the sudden realisation that you yourself could become disabled. This is a fundamental feature of the relations of disabled people with others. A white person does not feel a fear of becoming suddenly black and the source of racial prejudice is other than this. But everyone knows that accident and disease are always possibilities, and an encounter with a person with no arms, or no hearing, or a scarred face, vividly reminds us of the fragility of life. It is thus understandable that we defend ourselves from the shock of finitude, or the threat of being different. We all shrink from loss, and a disabled person is someone who has met loss, and lived through it.

AMG: Can we reflect further on the notion of the fear of loss. There are many ways in which people are born different – they are of a different gender, sexual orientation, race, skin colour, eye colour; they have different physical attributes and so on. Then there are other differences which are culturally or socially determined – nationality, social class, religion, access to wealth, education and other resources and so on. Many, but not all of these differences, underlie the inequalities and injustices that characterise our experience. The threat of the 'other' person who is different is often the fear that his 'gain' will be my 'loss'. Religion acts in this way; it is one of the principal ways in which we separate people into groups: Catholics, Jews and Muslims, the saved and the damned, the 'blessed' and the sinner. Biblically it is those whom God favours who possess the Promised Land, a land from which those not so favoured were driven. So my question is this – to what extent is my fear of the 'other' who is different a fear that they will possess what I possess?

JH: On the fear of loss: to what extent may my fear of the other be prompted by the fear that the other will take what I possess? Perhaps we might distinguish between the loss which is a gain to someone else, and the loss which is of no benefit to others. In the former case, the fear of loss is the fear of the other which might cause the loss but in the latter case, the fear is directed towards the loss itself. Nevertheless, we tend to treat the loss which does not benefit another as if it did, in an attempt to explain the loss, or to defend ourselves emotionally against it. For example, when William Shakespeare laments the effect of the passage of time upon his love, he writes as if time was a thief:

> Time will come and take my love away.
> This thought is as a death which cannot choose
> But weep to have that which it fears to lose.

When we miss something, we tend to look around suspiciously as if to discover who took it. This would make the loss intelligible; there would be someone to blame, and there might be the possibility of protest, of grabbing it back again. If we believe that we have a right to possess the things we have, then every loss will be regarded as a theft, and we look for the thief. So we may feel that death snatched the beloved away, or that Lady Luck did not smile upon our investments. It would follow that the greater our possessions, and the stronger our belief in our inalienable right to possess them, the greater our fear of loss, and the more suspicious we become towards possible causes of loss. This is one reason why rich people may tend to become individualised, living in large, isolated detached houses, separate from strangers, whereas poor people share what they have, live closely together in mutual dependence, with their social and cultural lives often marked by community celebration.

Religion is often interpreted as a coping strategy against loss, especially the loss of meaning. The psychology of religion associated with the Swiss academic Fritz Oser suggests that our basic religiosity appears in situations where we have to grapple with the unpredictable aspects of life in the presence of the divine, or whatever we take to be the ultimate. So, in a certain developmental stage, we may regard God as punishing or rewarding us for the way we have either broken or kept the commandments of God. At another stage of this development, we may evolve sophisticated ways of reconciling our sense of choice and freedom with our belief that God is shaping our lives.

Another religious response to the fear of loss is to deny that we possess anything by right. What do we have, asks the apostle, that we did not first receive? The Lord gave and the Lord has taken away; blessed be the name of the Lord. We brought nothing into this world, and can be sure that we shall take nothing out. Everything we possess is ours not by right but by grace. Therefore, when something appears to be taken away, instead of bitterness, the religious person may be conscious of a sense of gratitude that it was given at all, if only briefly. If life itself is a gift, then where, O death, is your sting? In some religious traditions, this way of dealing with loss is expressed in vows of poverty, in deliberately having nothing, or as little as possible, and in seeking to withdraw attachment from the things around us.

Not all the coping strategies of religion are as gracious. Religion can also support tribalism. In many species, males compete for females, and in some species, such as chimpanzees and humans, groups of males bond to compete with rival male groups. Human groups increase their sense of solidarity by sharing in myths and rituals which consolidate tribal affiliations and symbolise common loyalties. One of the most effective techniques of tribalisation is the distinguishing of 'us' from 'them'. 'We' speak a civilised language, but 'they' make primitive and meaningless sounds. 'We' are the free world but 'they' are slaves. 'We' are advanced but 'they' are less developed. Christianity seems to be full of such distinctions. Indeed, much Christian life seems to depend upon the creation of antitheses or dichotomies, in which one true belief, held by the people of God, is contrasted with a false belief held by the pagans. There are the 'saved' and the 'lost'; some go to heaven, others to hell. Those who believe are 'redeemed' but those who do not believe are 'damned'.

This then encourages us to reject the others as strangers, to fear them as not following our ways, and, probably, as wanting the pleasures and benefits of our superior life. Our fear of loss is thus focused by being projected onto the threatening others. The others will be subject to similar tendencies, and thus they may become really threatening and not merely imagined to be so. Fear of loss turns into conflict, and we call our armies our 'defence' forces, and our military strategies we describe as 'security' operations, and so they really may become.

Does Christian faith really need such distinctions? Must there be the 'saved' and the 'lost'? Must the pleasure of being saved be relished by the satisfaction of knowing that others are damned? Why should there not be universal salvation? In my own opinion, distinctions are necessary in the religious life in two senses. First, distinctions between the message and the surrounding static are necessary if communication is to be effective. We could not understand our conversation unless there was agreement about what was to be regarded as significant and what was to be relegated to the background as mere noise. In so far as Christian faith seeks to communicate a particular set of stories, values, rituals and beliefs, these must be communicated by contrast. Secondly, there is an ethical aspect of making such distinctions. Jesus spoke of the 'wide road' leading to destruction, and the many who walk it, and by contrast, of the 'narrow gate' leading to salvation and the few who find it. Jesus spoke of the poor who were blessed and the rich who would one day mourn. He contrasted the faithful bridesmaids who waited for the bridal party with the lazy ones who did not. The teaching of Jesus is full of such dichotomies, but they refer to the challenge of the ethical life, to the meaning of discipleship, and should not be turned into tribal preferences. There are references to goats and sheep, but the meaning is to challenge us to perceive Jesus Christ in the naked and the hungry, not to set up a tribal superiority, or to regard those who are not like us as being the goats. In other words, the alternatives set before people by Jesus were existential, not tribal. Jesus refuses us the ambiguity of procrastination and demands the urgency of the issues of life and death, our own life, our own death.

AMG: Finally, John, can I return to your comment about the way in which we project our fear of loss onto the 'other', the stranger. How does the stranger become the welcome guest?

JH: The ancient Hebrews were required to be hospitable towards strangers because they had also been strangers. They were to be merciful towards slaves because they themselves had once been slaves. In the story of the Lost Son, we know nothing about the previous history of the forgiving father. But I guess that he himself had been lost and found again when he was young, and this was one reason why he understood the desperation of the young man who came back to him asking for a job on the farm. The older brother had always been around the homestead. As the father said to him, 'Son, you are always with me, and everything I have is yours'. Exactly. It was just because the older brother was always there, taking for granted the security of the business, and had never been tempted to eat the scraps in the bin that he had no insight, and no capacity to receive his brother back.

Indeed, he turned his brother into a stranger, instead of recognising in this stranger his lost brother.

When we are told to forgive because we have been forgiven, the person who does not feel that he or she ever really needed forgiveness will not be able to forgive. This lies behind the comment of Jesus at the party when a working woman paid him more courtesy than his rich host. 'The one who is been much forgiven will be the one who loves the most.' So it is that when a supposed able-bodied person patronises, or is too loving towards a supposed disabled person, perhaps it is because there is a reluctance to admit one's own fragility, a defence against one's unacknowledged fear of loss. But the person who understands his or her inner vulnerability is conscious of inner fragility, has experienced failure and defeat, will be the one who will find it easiest to understand and accept the other.

So how does one learn to accept the stranger? By recognising that we also are strangers. This should be natural for those who follow the Christian way, for here we have no permanent city but look for the one to come. We are to live as pilgrims, as exiles, and therefore always to be open to those who in some other way are like us, pilgrims, exiles, refugees, strangers. When I was a stranger, you took me in; homeless, you gave me a home. When did we do these things for you, Lord? Every time you treat another person like this, it is myself you are so treating.

Note
1. John Hull would like to thank the Allan and Nesta Ferguson Trust, whose generous grant made possible the production of this text.